GREAT PEOPLE IN HISTORY

GREAT MATHEMATICIANS

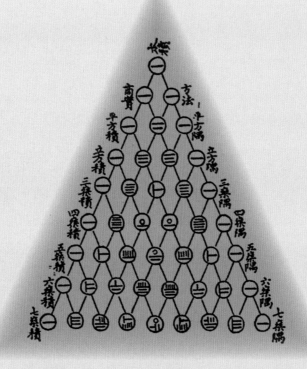

GREAT PEOPLE IN HISTORY

GREAT MATHEMATICIANS

Raymond Flood and Robin Wilson

ROSEN
PUBLISHING®
New York

Raymond Flood is an emeritus fellow and former vice president of Kellogg College, Oxford and was previously university lecturer in computing studies and mathematics at the Department for Continuing Education, Oxford University. His main research interests lie in statistics and the history of mathematics, and he was formerly president of the British Society for the History of Mathematics.

Robin Wilson is an emeritus professor of pure mathematics at the Open University, emeritus professor of geometry at Gresham College, London, and a former fellow of Keble College, Oxford. He currently teaches at Pembroke College, Oxford, and is president-elect of the British Society for the History of Mathematics. He is involved with the popularization and communication of mathematics and, in 2005, he was awarded a Pólya prize by the Mathematical Association of America for "outstanding expository writing."

This edition published in 2013 by:

The Rosen Publishing Group, Inc.
29 East 21st Street, New York, NY 10010

Library of Congress Cataloging-in-Publication Data

Flood, Raymond.
 Great mathematicians / Raymond Flood, Robin Wilson.
    pages cm. -- (Great people in history)
 Includes bibliographical references and index.
 ISBN 978-1-4777-0402-8 (library binding)
 1. Mathematicians--Biography--Juvenile literature. 2. Mathematics--History--Juvenile literature. I. Wilson, Robin J. II. Title.
 QA28.F55 2013
 510.92'2--dc23
 2012032367

Manufactured in China

SL002554US

CPSIA Compliance Information: Batch W13YA: For further information, contact Rosen Publishing, New York, New York, at 1-800-237-9932

Contents

ANCIENT MATHEMATICS

EARLY EUROPEAN MATHEMATICS

Introduction

This book aims to present mathematics "with a human face" and to celebrate its achievements in their historical context. It features a personal selection of many of the mathematicians whose lives and work interest us, presented with as little technical background as possible. Due to limitations of space and format, we have had to omit several mathematicians who we should have liked to include, and said less than we wished about those we have featured; but we hope you will find the result interesting and that it will whet your appetite for further research. This is not a book on the history of mathematics, which is a vast subject demanding a very different treatment. Our featured mathematicians are organized roughly chronologically. Throughout, we have tried to present the mathematicians in modern terminology and notation, so as to make them more accessible, and extracts have been translated into English rather than appearing in the original languages.

As the pages of this book will show, mathematics has always been a human endeavor as people have found themselves grappling with a wide range of problems, both practical and theoretical. The subject has as long and interesting a history as literature, music, or painting, and its origins were both international and multicultural.

For many who remember mathematics from their schooldays as a dull and dusty subject,

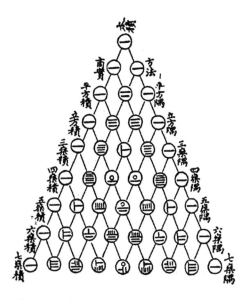

An arithmetical triangle (later known as Pascal's triangle) from Zhu Shijie's Siyuan yujian *(Precious Mirror of the Four Elements) of 1303*

largely incomprehensible and irrelevant to their everyday lives, this view of mathematics may come as a surprise. The subject has all too often been presented as a collection of rules to be learned and techniques to be applied, providing little understanding of the underlying principles or any appreciation of the nature of the subject as a whole—it is rather like teaching musical scales and intervals without ever playing a piece of music.

For wherever we look, mathematics pervades our daily lives. Credit cards and defense secrets are kept secure by encryption methods based on the properties of prime numbers, and mathematics is intimately involved when one flies in a plane, starts a car, switches on the television, forecasts the weather, books a holiday on the internet, programs a computer, navigates heavy traffic, analyzes a pile of statistical data, or seeks a cure for a disease. Without mathematics as its foundation there would be no science.

Mathematicians are often described as "pattern-searchers"—whether they study abstract patterns in numbers and shapes or look for symmetry in the natural world around us. Mathematical laws shape the patterns of seeds in sunflower heads and guide the solar system that we live in. Mathematics analyzes

William Blake's "Isaac Newton"

the minuscule structure of the atom and the massive extent of the universe.

But it can also be a great deal of fun. The logical thinking and problem-solving techniques that one learns in school can equally be put to recreational use. Chess is essentially a mathematical game, many people enjoy solving logical puzzles based on mathematical ideas, and thousands enjoy solving sudoku puzzles in print or on their cell phones, a pastime arising from combinatorial mathematics.

Mathematics is developing at an ever-increasing rate—indeed, more new mathematics has been discovered since World War II than was known up to that time. An outcome of all this activity has been the International Congresses of Mathematicians, which are held every four years for the presentation and discussion of the latest advances in the field.

But none of this would have happened if it had not been for the mathematicians who created their subject.

In this book you will meet time-measurers like the Mayans and Huygens, logicians like Aristotle and Russell, geometers like Apollonius and Lobachevsky, statisticians like Bernoulli and Nightingale, arithmeticians like Pythagoras and al-Khwarizmi, and calculators like Napier and Babbage. We will introduce you to the number-theorist Fermat, the applied mathematician Poisson, the textbook writer Euclid, the astronomer Ptolemy, and the algebraist Galois. We hope you find all their lives and achievements as fascinating as we do.

Wherever we look, mathematics pervades our daily lives.

ANCIENT MATHEMATICS

Mathematics is ancient and multicultural. Several examples of early counting devices on bone (such as tally sticks) have survived, and some of the earliest examples of writing (from around 5000 BCE) were financial accounts involving numbers. Much mathematical thought and ingenuity also went into the construction of such edifices as the Great Pyramids of Egypt, the stone circles of Stonehenge, England, and the Parthenon in Athens.

In this chapter we describe the mathematical contributions of several ancient cultures: Egypt, Mesopotamia, Greece, China, India, and Central America. The mathematics developed in each culture depended on need, which may have been practically inspired (for example, agricultural, administrative, financial, or military), academically motivated (educational or philosophical), or a mixture of both.

SOURCE MATERIAL

Much of what we know about a particular culture depends on the availability of appropriate primary source material.

For the Mesopotamians we have many thousands of mathematical clay tablets that provide much useful information. On the other hand, the Egyptians and the Greeks wrote on papyrus, made from reeds that rarely survive the ravages of the centuries, although we do have two substantial Egyptian mathematical papyri and a handful of Greek extracts. The Chinese wrote their mathematics on bamboo and paper, little of which has survived. The Mayans wrote on stone pillars called *stelae,* which contain useful material. They also produced codices, made of bark paper; a handful of these survive, but most were destroyed during the Spanish Conquest many centuries later.

A Mesopotamian clay tablet

Apart from this, we have to rely on commentaries and translations. For the classical Greek writings we have commentaries by a few later Greek mathematicians, and also a substantial number of Arabic translations and commentaries by Islamic scholars. There are also later translations into Latin, though how true these may be to the original works remains a cause for speculation.

COUNTING SYSTEMS

All civilizations needed to be able to count, whether for simple household purposes or for more substantial activities such as the construction of buildings or the planting of fields.

As we shall see, the number systems developed by different cultures varied considerably. The Egyptians used a decimal system with different symbols for 1, 10, 100, 1,000, etc. The Greeks used different Greek letters for the units from 1 to 9, the tens from 10 to 90, and the hundreds from 100 to 900. Other cultures developed place-value counting systems with a limited number of symbols: here the same symbol may play different roles, such as the two 3s in 3,835 (referring to 3,000 and 30). The Chinese used a decimal place-value system, while the Mesopotamians had a system based on 60 and the Mayans developed a system mainly based on 20.

Any place-value system needs the concept of zero; for example, we write 207, with a zero in the tens place, to distinguish it from 27. Sometimes the positioning of a zero was clear from the context. At other times a gap was left, as in the Chinese counting boards, or a zero symbol was specifically designed, as in the Mayan system.

The use of zero in a decimal place-value system eventually emerged in India and elsewhere, and rules were given for calculating with it. The Indian counting system was later developed by Islamic mathematicians and gave rise to what we now call the *Hindu–Arabic numerals*, the system we use today.

So, starting from the natural numbers, 1, 2, 3, … , generations of mathematicians obtained all the *integers*—the positive and negative whole numbers and zero. This was a lengthy process that took thousands of years to accomplish.

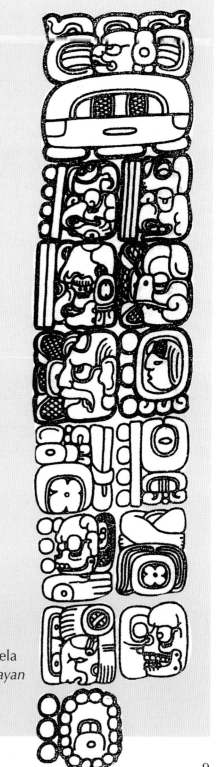

A Central American stela *featuring Mayan head-form numbers*

The Egyptians

The magnificent pyramids of Giza, dating from about 2600 BCE, attest to the Egyptians' extremely accurate measuring ability. In particular, the Great Pyramid of Cheops, constructed from over two million blocks averaging around 2 tons in weight, is an impressive 460 feet (140 meters) high and has a square base whose sides of length 755 feet (230 m) agree to within less than 0.01 percent.

Our knowledge of later Egyptian mathematics is scanty, and comes mainly from two primary sources: the 16-foot-long (5-m) "Rhind papyrus" (*c.*1650 BCE), named after its Victorian purchaser Henry Rhind and housed in the British Museum, and the "Moscow papyrus" (*c.*1850 BCE), currently housed in a Moscow museum.

These papyri include tables of fractions and several dozen solved problems in arithmetic and geometry. Such exercises were used in the training of scribes, and range from division problems involving the sharing of loaves in specified proportions to those requiring the volume of a cylindrical granary of given diameter and height.

THE EGYPTIAN COUNTING SYSTEM

The Egyptians used a decimal system, but wrote different symbols (called *hieroglyphs*) for 1 (a vertical rod), 10 (a heel bone), 100 (a coiled rope), 1,000 (a lotus flower), etc.

Below: *The pyramids at Giza*

| 1 | 10 | 100 | 1000 |

Each number appeared with the appropriate repetitions of each symbol, written from right to left; for example, the number 2,658 was:

The Egyptians calculated with *unit fractions* (or reciprocals), fractions with 1 in the numerator such as 1/8, 1/52 or 1/104 (they also used the fraction 2/3); for example, they wrote 1/8 1/52 1/104 instead of 2/13, since 1/8 + 1/52 + 1/104 = 2/13.

To aid such calculations, the Rhind papyrus includes a table of unit fractions for each of the fractions 2/5, 2/7, 2/9, ... , 2/101.

The remarkable ability of the Egyptians to calculate with these unit fractions can be

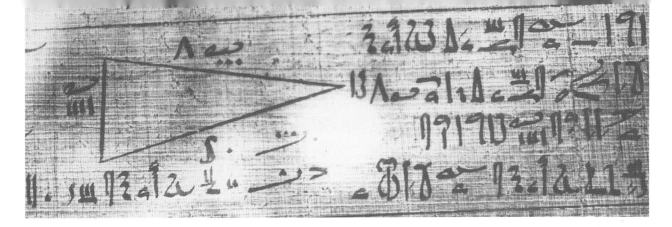

Above: *Part of the Rhind papyrus*

witnessed in Problem 31 of the Rhind papyrus:

> *A quantity, its ²/₃, its ½ and its ¹/₇, added together become 33. What is the quantity?*

To solve this problem with our modern algebraic notation, we would call the unknown quantity x and obtain the equation:

$$x + {}^{2}/_{3}x + {}^{1}/_{2}x + {}^{1}/_{7}x = 33$$

We would then solve this equation to give:

$$x = 14{}^{28}/_{97}$$

But the answer the Egyptians gave, expressed with unit fractions, was:

$$14¼ \; {}^{1}/_{56} \; {}^{1}/_{97} \; {}^{1}/_{194} \; {}^{1}/_{388} \; {}^{1}/_{679} \; {}^{1}/_{776}$$

A truly impressive feat of calculation.

DISTRIBUTION PROBLEMS

Several problems on the Rhind papyrus involve the distribution of some commodity, such as bread or beer. For example, Problem 65 asks:

> *Example of dividing 100 loaves among 10 men, including a boatman, a foreman, and a doorkeeper, who each receive a double share. What is the share of each?*

To solve this, the scribe replaced each man receiving a double share by two people:

> *The working out: add to the number of men 3 for those with double portions; it makes 13. Multiply 13 so as to get 100; the result is 7²/₃ ¹/₃₉. This then is the ration for seven of the men, the boatman, the foreman, and the doorkeeper receiving double shares [= 15¹/₃ ¹/₂₆ ¹/₇₈].*

The Area of a Circle

Several problems in the Rhind papyrus involve circles of a given diameter. You may recall that:

> The area of a circle of radius r is πr^2.

Since the diameter $d = 2r$, this area can also be written as $\frac{1}{4}\pi d^2$. The number that we now denote by π also appears in the formula for the circumference:

> The circumference of a circle of radius r and diameter d is $2\pi r = \pi d$.

The value of π is about ²²/₇ (= 3¹/₇), and a more accurate approximation is 3.1415926; however, π cannot be written down exactly as its decimal expansion goes on for ever.

Problem 50 of the Rhind papyrus asks for the area of a circle of diameter 9:

> Example of a round field of diameter 9 khet. What is its area?
>
> Answer: Take away ¹/₉ of the diameter, namely 1; the remainder is 8. Multiply 8 times 8; it makes 64. Therefore it contains 64 setat of land.

The Egyptians found by experience that they could approximate the area of a circle with diameter d by reducing d by one-ninth and squaring the result. So here, where $d = 9$, they reduced d by one-ninth (giving 8) and then squared the result (giving 64).

Their method corresponds to a value of π of 3¹³/₈₁, which is about 3.16, within 1 percent of the correct value.

The Mesopotamians

Mesopotamian (or Babylonian) mathematics developed over some three thousand years and over a wide region, but the problems we consider here date mainly from the Old Babylonian period (around 1800 BCE). The word Mesopotamian *comes from the Greek for "between the rivers" and refers to the area between the rivers Tigris and Euphrates in modern-day Iraq.*

The primary source material is very different in form and content from that of the Egyptians of the same period. Using a wedge-shaped stylus, the Mesopotamians imprinted their symbols into moist clay—this is called *cuneiform writing*—and the tablet was then left to harden in the sun. Many thousands of mathematical clay tablets have survived.

THE SEXAGESIMAL SYSTEM

We write numbers in the decimal place-value system, based on 10, with separate columns for units, tens, hundreds, etc., as we move from right to left. Each place has value ten times the next; for example, 3,235 means:

$$(3 \times 1,000) + (2 \times 100) + (3 \times 10) + (5 \times 1)$$

The Mesopotamians also used a place-value system, but it was a "sexagesimal" system, based on 60: each place has value sixty times the next. It used two symbols, which we write here as Y for 1 and < for 10:

- for 32 they wrote <<<YY;

- for 870 they wrote <YYYY   <<<,
  since 870 = 840 + 24 = (14 × 60) + 30;

- for 8,492 they wrote YY   <<Y   <<<YY,
  since 8,492 = (2 × 60²) + (21 × 60) + 32.

Remnants of their sexagesimal system survive in our measurements of time (60 seconds in a minute, 60 minutes in an hour) and of angles. The Mesopotamians developed the ability to calculate with large sexagesimal numbers, and used them to chart the cycles of the moon and construct a reliable calendar.

TYPES OF TABLET

There were essentially three types of mathematical clay tablet. Some of them list tables of numbers for use in calculations and are called *table tablets*: an example of a table tablet is the 9-times multiplication table below.

Other clay tablets, known as *problem tablets*, contain posed and solved mathematical problems. A third type may be described as *rough work*, which were created by students while learning.

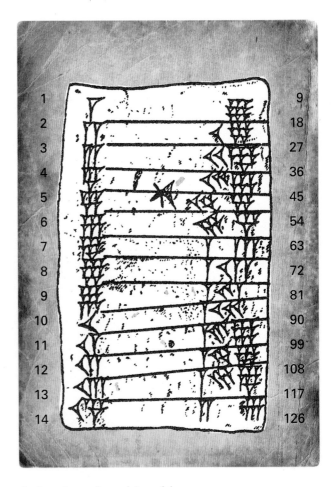

A drawing of a table tablet

The Square Root of 2

A particularly unusual tablet, which illustrates the Mesopotamians' remarkable ability to calculate with great accuracy, depicts a square with its two diagonals and the sexagesimal numbers 30, 1;24,51,10 and 42;25,35. These numbers refer to the side of the square (of length 30), the square root of 2, and the diagonal (of length 30√2).

The amazing accuracy of their value for the square root:

1;24,51,10

$= 1 + {}^{24}/_{60} + {}^{51}/_{3600} + {}^{10}/_{216000}$

(= 1.4142128... in decimal notation)

becomes apparent if we square it—we get:

1;59,59,59,38,1,40

(= 1.999995... in decimal notation)

This differs from 2 by about 5 parts in a million.

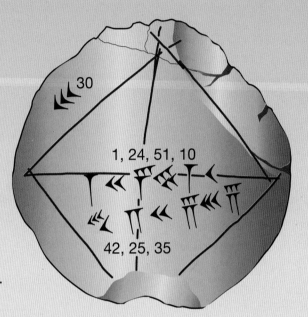

An example of a Mesopotamian problem is the following, on the weight of a stone: it appears on a clay tablet featuring twenty-three problems of the same type, suggesting that it may have been used for teaching purposes.

I found a stone, but did not weigh it; after I weighed out 8 times its weight, added 3 gin, and added one-third of one-thirteenth multiplied by 21, I weighed it: 1 ma-na. What was the original weight of the stone? The original weight was 4⅓ gin.

This problem is clearly not a practical one—if we want the weight of the stone, why don't we just weigh it? Unfortunately, we do not know how the scribe solved the problem—we just have the answer.

Our next example is more complicated, and is one of a dozen similar problems on the same tablet:

I have subtracted the side of my square from the area: 14,30. You write down 1, the coefficient. You break off half of 1. 0;30 and 0;30 you multiply. You add 0;15 to 14,30. Result 14,30;15.

This is the square of 29;30. You add 0;30, which you multiplied, to 29;30. Result: 30, the side of the square.

This is a quadratic equation: $x^2 - x = 870$, in modern algebraic notation. Here, x is the side of the square, x^2 is the area, and 14;30 is our decimal number 870. The steps of the above solution give, successively:

1, ½, (½)² = ¼, 870¼, 29½, 30

The method in this example is called "completing the square" and is essentially the one we use today, four thousand years later.

Thales

Little is known about Thales (c.624–c.546 BCE). According to legend, he came from the Greek Ionian city of Miletus on the west coast of Asia Minor in modern-day Turkey. Many claims have been made for him: he visited Egypt and calculated the height of the pyramids, predicted a solar eclipse in 585 BCE, showed how rubbing feathers with a stone produces electricity, and originated the phrase "know thyself."

Thales is widely considered the first important Greek mathematician. Bertrand Russell claimed that "Western philosophy begins with Thales," and indeed Thales is widely held to be one of the Seven Sages of Greece, a title awarded by tradition to seven outstanding Greek philosophers from the sixth century BCE.

GREEK MATHEMATICAL SOURCES

Unlike Ancient Egypt, where there are a few well-preserved papyri, and Mesopotamia where many thousands of clay tablets survive, we have very few Greek primary sources. As in Egypt, the Greeks wrote on papyrus, which did not survive the centuries; and there were disasters, such as a library fire at Alexandria, in which many of the primary sources perished.

The Seven Sages of Greece: a woodcut from The Nuremberg Chronicle *(1493); Thales is pictured on the left.*

So we have to rely mainly on commentaries and later versions. The best-known commentator on Greek mathematics was Proclus (fifth century CE), who supposedly derived his material from earlier commentaries (now lost) by Eudemus of Rhodes (fourth century BCE). But Proclus lived a thousand years after Thales, so we should treat his commentaries with caution, while acknowledging that they are all we have.

GEOMETRY

The mathematical style developed by the early Greeks differed markedly from anything that went before. Of their many contributions to mathematics, and to geometry in particular, the ideas of deductive reasoning and mathematical proof are the most fundamental. Starting with some initial assumptions, known as *axioms* or *postulates*, they made simple deductions, then more complicated ones, and so on, eventually deriving a great hierarchy of results, each depending on previous ones.

THE THEOREMS OF THALES

A number of geometrical results have been ascribed to Thales by various commentators:

THE ANGLE IN A SEMICIRCLE
If AB is a diameter of a circle, and if P is any other point on the circle, then the angle APB is a right angle.

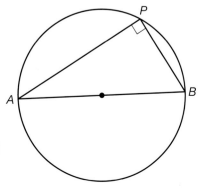

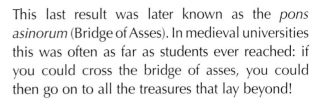

THE INTERCEPT THEOREM

Let two lines intersect at a point P, and let two parallel lines cut these lines in the points A, B and C, D, as shown below. Then PA / AB = PC / CD.

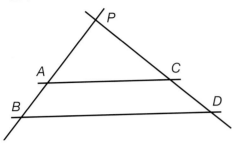

THE BASE ANGLES OF AN ISOSCELES TRIANGLE

A triangle is *isosceles* if two of its sides are equal. The commentator Eudemus attributed to Thales the discovery that: *The base angles of an isosceles triangle are equal.*

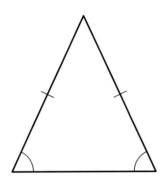

This last result was later known as the *pons asinorum* (Bridge of Asses). In medieval universities this was often as far as students ever reached: if you could cross the bridge of asses, you could then go on to all the treasures that lay beyond!

Thales of Miletus

Proof by Contradiction

In their geometry the Greeks used various methods of proof. For the following result, Thales gave a *proof by contradiction* (or *reductio ad absurdum*), where he assumed the desired result to be false and then deduced a consequence that contradicted this assumption—so the result is true.

ANY CIRCLE IS BISECTED BY ITS DIAMETER

While writing about Euclid's *Elements*, Proclus remarked:

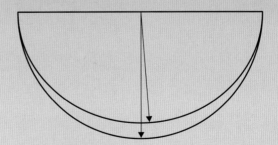

The famous Thales is said to have been the first to demonstrate that the circle is bisected by the diameter.

If you wish to demonstrate this mathematically, imagine the diameter drawn and one part of the circle fitted upon the other.

If it is not equal to the other, it will fall either inside or outside it, and in either case it will follow that a shorter line is equal to a longer. For all the lines from the center to the circumference are equal, and hence the line that extends beyond will be equal to the line that falls short, which is impossible.

This contradiction proves the result.

Pythagoras

The semi-legendary figure of Pythagoras (c.570–490 BCE) was born on the island of Samos, in the Aegean Sea. In his youth he studied mathematics, astronomy, philosophy, and music. Possibly around 520 BCE, he left Samos to go to the Greek seaport of Crotona (now in Southern Italy) and formed a philosophical school, now known as the Pythagoreans.

The inner members of the Pythagoreans (the *mathematikoi*) apparently obeyed a strict regime, having no personal possessions and eating only vegetables and beans; the sect was open to both men and women.

The Pythagoreans studied mathematics, astronomy, and philosophy. They believed that *everything is created from whole numbers*, and that anything worthy of study can be quantified. They are said to have subdivided the mathematical sciences into four parts: *arithmetic, geometry, astronomy,* and *music* (later called the *quadrivium*). These subjects, in combination with

Pythagoras, from Raphael's fresco The School of Athens

NUMBER PATTERNS

For the Pythagoreans, "arithmetic" meant studying whole numbers, which they sometimes represented geometrically; for example, they considered *square numbers* as being formed by square patterns of dots or pebbles.

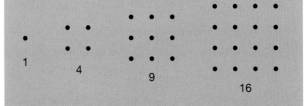

Using such pictures they could show that square numbers can be obtained by adding consecutive odd numbers, starting from 1, for example:

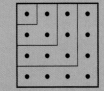

$$16 = 1 + 3 + 5 + 7$$

They also studied *triangular numbers*, formed by triangular patterns of dots. The first few triangular numbers are:

1, 3, 6, 10, 15 and 21

Notice that: 3 = 1 + 2, 6 = 1 + 2 + 3,
        10 = 1 + 2 + 3 + 4, etc.

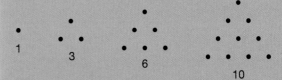

Using such pictures they could show that the sum of any two consecutive triangular numbers is a square number, for example:

$$10 + 15 = 25$$

The Pythagorean Theorem

Important in geometry are *right-angled triangles*, where one of the angles is 90°; an example is the triangle with sides 3, 4, 5.

The most important result concerning them is known as the *Pythagorean theorem*, although no contemporary historical evidence links it to Pythagoras himself. Although it was known by the Mesopotamians a thousand years earlier, the Greeks were probably the first to prove it.

Geometrically, the Pythagorean theorem says that if we take a right-angled triangle and draw squares on each side of it, then:

> *The area of the square on the longest side is equal to the sum of the areas of the squares on the other two sides*

—that is, (area of Z) = (area of X) + (area of Y)

So, for a right-angled triangle with sides of lengths *a*, *b*, and *c* (where *c* is the length of the longest side), we have $a^2 + b^2 = c^2$ —for example, for the triangle with sides 3, 4, 5:

$$3^2 + 4^2 = 9 + 16 = 25 = 5^2$$

Other examples are the right-angled triangles with sides 5, 12, 13 and 8, 15, 17.

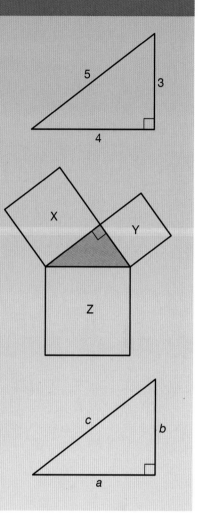

the *trivium* (the liberal arts of grammar, rhetoric, and logic), comprised the "liberal arts"—the curriculum of academies and universities over the next two thousand years.

MATHEMATICS AND MUSIC

The Pythagoreans also experimented with music—in particular, linking certain musical intervals to simple ratios between small numbers.

It is likely that they discovered these ratios by plucking strings of different lengths and comparing the notes produced; for example, the harmonious interval of an *octave* results from halving the length of a string, giving a frequency ratio of 2 to 1, while another harmonious interval, a *perfect fifth*, results from stopping a string at two-thirds of its length, giving a ratio of 3 to 2.

Right: *This woodcut from 1492 features some of Pythagoras's musical experiments.*

Plato and Aristotle

From about 500 to 300 BCE, Athens became the most important intellectual center in Greece, numbering among its scholars Socrates, Plato (429–347 BCE), and Aristotle (384–322 BCE). Although neither Plato nor Aristotle is remembered primarily as a mathematician, both helped to set the stage for the "golden age of Greek mathematics" in Alexandria.

PLATO'S ACADEMY

The next great era of Greek mathematics was centered on Athens, with the founding of Plato's Academy around 387 BCE in a suburb of Athens called "Academy" (from which it derived its name). Here Plato wrote and directed studies, and the Academy soon became the focal point for mathematical and philosophical activities.

Plato believed that the study of these subjects provided the finest training for those who were to hold positions of responsibility in the state, and in his *Republic* he discussed at length the importance for the "philosopher-ruler" of each of the four mathematical arts—arithmetic, geometry, astronomy, and music. Significantly, over the entrance appeared the inscription:

Let no one ignorant of geometry enter here.

THE PLATONIC SOLIDS

Plato's book *Timaeus* is also of mathematical interest and includes a discussion of the five regular solids: *tetrahedron, cube, octahedron, dodecahedron,* and *icosahedron.*

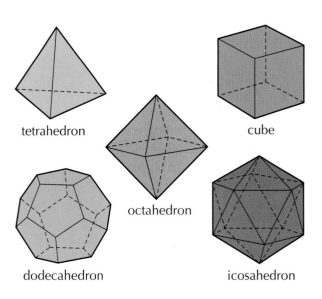

tetrahedron

cube

octahedron

dodecahedron

icosahedron

The five regular solids

Plato and Aristotle, from Raphael's fresco
The School of Athens

In these solid figures (or *polyhedra*, meaning "many-faced"), the faces are all regular polygons of the same type (triangles, squares, or pentagons) and the arrangement of polygons at each corner is the same: for example, the cube has six square faces with three of them meeting at each corner, and the icosahedron has twenty triangular faces with five meeting at each corner.

In his *Timaeus*, Plato linked the universe with the dodecahedron and assigned the other four polyhedra to the Greek elements of earth, air, fire, and water. As a result, the regular polyhedra are often called *Platonic solids*.

SOCRATES AND THE SLAVE BOY

In his short dialogue *Meno*, Plato describes how Socrates drew in the sand a square of side 2 and area 4. He then asked a slave boy how to draw a square with double the area (8).

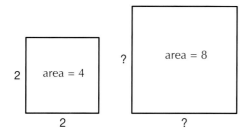

The boy first suggested doubling the side of the square to 4, but that gave four times the area (16). He then proposed a square with side 3, but that area was also too large (9). Eventually, after much discussion, he settled on the square based on the *diagonal* of the original square; this has area 8, as required.

The *Meno* dialogue is a wonderful example of teaching by asking questions, and was far removed from anything previously seen in Egypt or Mesopotamia.

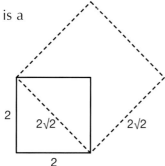

ARISTOTLE

Aristotle became a student at the Academy at the age of seventeen and stayed there for some twenty years until Plato's death.

He was fascinated by logical questions and systematized the study of logic and deductive reasoning. In particular, he studied the nature of mathematical proof and considered deductions (known as *syllogisms*), such as:

All men are mortal,
Socrates is a man,
Therefore Socrates is mortal.

Aristotle also alluded to a proof that the ratio of the diagonal of a square to its side (that is, $\sqrt{2}$) cannot be written in fraction form p/q, where p and q are whole numbers.

Why $\sqrt{2}$ Cannot be Written as a Fraction p/q

The proof is by contradiction: we assume that $\sqrt{2}$ *can* be written as a fraction p/q, and show that this leads to a contradiction.

- We can assume that this fraction is written in its lowest terms—that is, p and q have no common factor (other than 1).

- By squaring, we can rewrite the equation $\sqrt{2} = p/q$ as $2 = p^2/q^2$, and so $p^2 = 2q^2$. This means that p^2 must be an even number (because it is twice q^2), and so p must also be even (because if p were odd, then p^2 would also be odd).

- Since p is even, we can write $p = 2k$, for some whole number k. So $p^2 = 2q^2 = 4k^2$, which gives $q^2 = 2k^2$. It follows that q^2 is an even number, so q is also even.

- But this gives the required contradiction: p and q are both even, so both have a factor of 2. This contradicts the fact that p and q have no common factor.

The contradiction arises from our original assumption that $\sqrt{2}$ can be written as a fraction p/q—so this assumption must be wrong: $\sqrt{2}$ cannot be written as a fraction.

Euclid

Around 300 BCE, with the rise to power of Ptolemy I, mathematical activity moved to the Egyptian part of the Greek empire. In Alexandria, Ptolemy founded a university that became the intellectual center for Greek scholarship for over eight hundred years. He also started its famous library, which eventually held over half-a-million manuscripts before being destroyed by fire. Alexandria's Pharos lighthouse was one of the seven wonders of the ancient world.

THE *ELEMENTS*

The first important mathematician associated with Alexandria was Euclid (c.300 BCE), who is credited with writing on geometry, optics, and astronomy. But he is mainly remembered for one work—the *Elements*, the most influential and widely read mathematical book of all time. It was in use for more than two thousand years and, apart from the Bible, may even be the most printed book ever.

Euclid's *Elements*, a model of deductive reasoning, was a compilation of known results organized in a logical order. Starting from initial axioms and postulates, it used rules of deduction to derive each new proposition in a systematic way. It was not the earliest such work, but was the most important.

It consists of thirteen sections, usually called "Books" although they were written on rolls of papyrus. They are traditionally divided into three main parts—plane geometry, arithmetic, and solid geometry.

PLANE GEOMETRY

The geometrical part (Books I to VI) opens with definitions of such basic terms as *point*, *line*, and *circle*, followed by some axioms (or postulates) that permit us to carry out certain geometrical constructions with an unmarked ruler and a pair of compasses. These include:

• drawing a straight line from any given point to any other,

• drawing a circle with any given center and radius.

Euclid then presented his first result, which gives a construction for an equilateral triangle (a triangle with all three sides equal):

> *Given a straight line AB, construct an equilateral triangle with AB as its base.*

To do this, he used the second construction above to draw two circles, one with center *A* and radius *AB*, and the other with center *B* and radius *AB*. These circles meet at two points *C* and *D*, and the triangle *ABC* (or *ABD*) is then the required equilateral triangle.

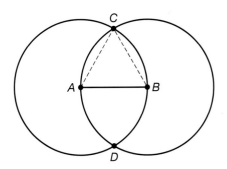

Euclid explained why this construction always gives an equilateral triangle. At each stage of his proof he made reference to an appropriate definition or postulate.

Book I continues with results about congruent triangles (those of the same size and shape) and parallel lines. Euclid also proved the "angle-sum theorem":

> *The angles of any triangle add up to 180°,*

and thereby gave a proof of the Pythagorean theorem.

Book II includes various results on rectangles, such as the construction of a rectangle equal in

Solid Geometry

The final three books of Euclid's *Elements* deal with aspects of three-dimensional geometry. Of these, Book XIII is the most remarkable. Here, Euclid investigated the five regular solids (tetrahedron, cube, octahedron, dodecahedron, and icosahedron) and showed how they can be constructed.

He concluded the *Elements* by proving that these are the only possible regular solids—there can be no others. This, the first ever "classification theorem" in mathematics, forms a fitting climax to this great work.

area to a given triangle, while Book III introduces properties of circles, such as Thales' theorem on the angle in a semicircle, and a proof that

If a quadrilateral is drawn in a circle then the opposite angles add up to 180°.

$$a + c = 180°$$
$$b + d = 180°$$

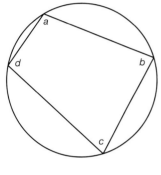

Book IV contains circle constructions, including those of regular 5-sided, 6-sided, and 15-sided polygons inside a given circle.

Book V may be due to Eudoxus, a student of Plato at the Academy, and concerns ratios of lengths: an example in modern notation is:

If $a / b = c / d$, then $a / c = b / d$.

These are then applied in Book VI to similar geometrical figures (those of the same shape but not necessarily the same size).

ARITHMETIC

In Books VII to IX, we enter the world of arithmetic, but the descriptions are still given in geometrical terms, using lengths of lines to represent numbers. There are discussions of odd and even numbers, and of what it means for one number to be a factor of another. Included here is the so-called *Euclidean algorithm*, a systematic method for finding the highest common factor of two numbers.

Right: Euclid is shown presenting his Elements *to King Ptolemy I Soter in Alexandria in this illustration by Louis Figuier, 1866.*

This section of the *Elements* also includes a discussion of prime numbers. A *prime number* is a number, greater than 1, whose only factors are itself and 1: the first few are:

2, 3, 5, 7, 11, 13, 17, 19, 23, and 29

They are central to arithmetic because they are the building blocks for numbers: every whole number can be obtained by multiplying prime numbers—for example:

$126 = 2 \times 3 \times 3 \times 7$

Book IX contains Euclid's proof of the fact that the list of primes continues for ever:

There are infinitely many prime numbers.

It is one of the most famous proofs in the whole of mathematics.

Archimedes

Archimedes (c.287–212 BCE), a native of Syracuse on the island of Sicily and one of the greatest mathematicians of all time, worked over a wide range of areas. In geometry he calculated the surface areas and volumes of various solids, listed the "semi-regular solids," investigated spirals, and estimated the value of π. In applied mathematics he contributed to hydrostatics and discovered the law of the lever.

TWO STORIES

Archimedes is mainly known for two stories, recounted some two hundred years later and of doubtful authenticity.

The first was recalled by the Roman writer Vitruvius. Archimedes' friend King Hiero wished to find whether his crown was of pure gold or whether it was partially made of silver. Archimedes discovered the key to solving this problem while getting into a bath and observing that the more his body sank into it, the more water flowed over the edge. Overjoyed at his discovery, he jumped out of his bath and ran home naked shouting "Eureka!" (or more accurately "Heureka!")— I have found it!

The other story, presented by Plutarch, concerns Archimedes' untimely death at the hand of a Roman soldier. In 212 BCE, during the siege of Syracuse, Archimedes was engrossed in a mathematical problem, unaware that the city had been captured, when the soldier came up and threatened to kill him. Archimedes begged him to wait until he had completed his calculations, whereupon the soldier flew into a rage and slew him on the spot.

TWO APPLICATIONS

Archimedes contributed to many areas of mathematics, and seems to be one of the few Greek mathematicians interested in its applications.

In hydrostatics, *Archimedes' principle* is that the weight of an object immersed in water is reduced by an amount equal to the weight of water displaced. Archimedes also devised ingenious mechanical weapons of war for the defense of Syracuse and is credited with inventing the Archimedean screw, a device for for raising water from a river.

Another result of his was the law of the lever— that if weights W_1 and W_2 are placed at the ends of a balance, then they are in equilibrium at distances a and b that are inversely proportional to the weights:

$$W_1 \times a = W_2 \times b$$

Archimedes, *by Georg Andreas Böckler, 1661*

GEOMETRY

But Archimedes did not only work on applications. Among his best-known geometrical results are:

- determinations of the centers of gravity of triangles, parallelograms, and hemispheres,

- some work on spirals, including one now known as the *Archimedean spiral,*

- impressive calculations of the volumes of spheres, cones, and cylinders, such as his celebrated result (which he wanted engraved on his tomb) that *the volume of a cylinder is 1½ times that of the sphere it surrounds.*

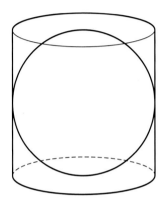

Archimedes also investigated the "semi-regular" polyhedra, in which the faces are regular polygons but are not all the same; for example, a truncated icosahedron (or soccer ball) is made up of regular pentagons and hexagons. Archimedes found that there are just thirteen such solids: they are now known as the *Archimedean polyhedra.*

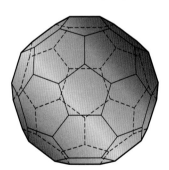

A truncated icosahedron and a soccer ball

COUNTING GRAINS OF SAND

In arithmetic, Archimedes wrote *The Sand-Reckoner* to refute the prevalent idea that the number of grains of sand in the universe is infinite. To this end, he first investigated the number $100,000,000^{100,000,000}$, which he called P, and then proceeded to construct the number $p^{100,000,000}$. As he carefully explained, this massive number is finite, yet exceeds the number of grains of sand in the universe. Since the Greek number system had names for numbers up to a myriad (10,000) and no further, this was a remarkable achievement.

Circle Measurement

One of Archimedes' best-known results concerns the ratio of a circle's circumference to its diameter (that is, π).

He began by drawing hexagons inside and outside a circle and compared their perimeters with the circumference of the circle: this tells us that π lies between 3 and 3.464.

He then replaced the hexagon by a 12-sided polygon and recalculated the lengths.

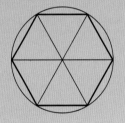
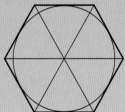
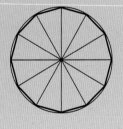
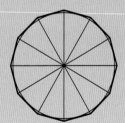

Continuing in this way, and performing the calculations for polygons with 24, 48, and 96 sides, without actually drawing them, he concluded that (in our notation):

$$3 \tfrac{10}{71} < \pi < 3\tfrac{1}{7}$$

this gives a value for π of about 3.14, which is correct to two decimal places.

As we shall see, this method was refined over the next two thousand years to yield the value of π to many decimal places.

Apollonius

Back in Alexandria, Apollonius of Perga (c.262–c.190 BCE), known since antiquity as "the Great Geometer," was writing his celebrated treatise on conics: these curves are of three different types—an ellipse (with a circle as a special case), a parabola, and a hyperbola. Apollonius's Conics *was a veritable tour de force, but it is not an easy work to read.*

THREE TYPES OF CONIC

The conic sections are generally considered to have been discovered by Menaechmus, a pupil of Eudoxus. By slicing a cone in various ways, he could obtain the following curves:

- slicing it horizontally gives a *circle*
- slicing it at a slant gives an *ellipse*
- slicing it parallel to the side of the cone gives a *parabola*
- slicing it vertically gives a *hyperbola*

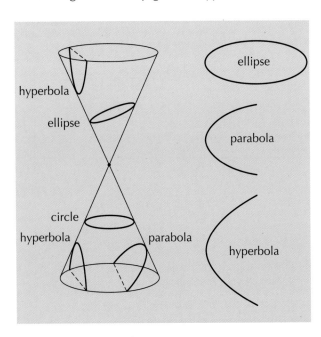

Slicing a cone

These curves can also be obtained by taking a fixed point (the *focus*) and a fixed line (the *directrix*) and letting a point *P* move so that its distances from them are in a fixed ratio *r*. For $r = 1$ we have a parabola; for $r < 1$ we have an ellipse; for $r > 1$ we have a hyperbola.

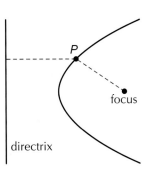

The focus–directrix definition of a parabola

Another way to draw an ellipse (used by gardeners to make elliptical flower beds) is to tie a rope to two pegs and trace out the curve.

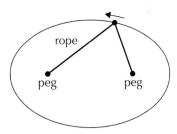

APOLLONIUS'S CONICS

While still a young man, Apollonius traveled to Alexandria to study with the followers of Euclid. He remained there, teaching and writing a number of geometrical works, the most influential of which was his monumental treatise on Conics. This appeared in eight parts: the early ones contain basic material, much of it previously known, while later ones present some stunningly original results.

Most of what we know about Apollonius's life appears in the letters that preface the eight parts: it is here we learn that he made visits to Pergamum and Ephesus to discuss his work with fellow geometers.

Two Later Editions of Apollonius's Conics

After the invention of printing in the fifteenth century, many Greek writings appeared in book form. Here we see a sixteenth-century edition of the *Conics*, and the frontispiece of a 1710 edition by Edmond Halley (of "Halley's comet" fame). The latter depicts the Greek philosopher Aristippus, shipwrecked with his fearful colleagues on the island of Rhodes; on noticing some geometrical figures drawn in the sand, Aristippus exclaimed "Let us be of good cheer, for I see the traces of man."

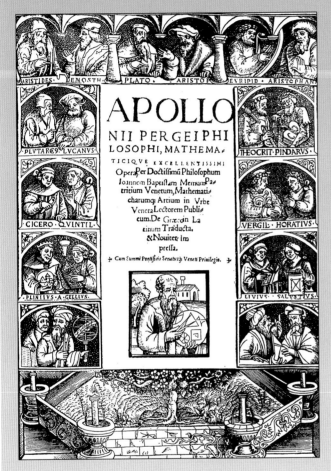

A sixteenth-century edition

Halley's 1710 edition

THE CIRCLE OF APOLLONIUS

One of Apollonius's most famous results is known as the circle of Apollonius:

Suppose that a point P moves in the plane so that its distance from a point A is in a fixed ratio (≠ 1) to its distance from a point B. Then the point traces out a circle.

The diagram opposite shows the circle traced out when the point P is always twice as far from A as it is from B.

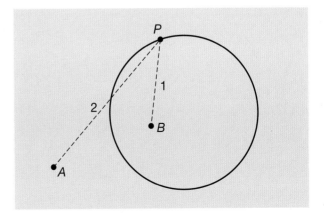

The circle of Apollonius

Hipparchus and Ptolemy

The first trigonometrical approach to astronomy was made by Hipparchus (190–120 BCE), sometimes called "the Father of Trigonometry." Possibly the greatest astronomical observer of antiquity, he discovered the precession of the equinoxes, produced the first known star catalog, and constructed a "table of chords" yielding the sines of angles. Claudius Ptolemy of Alexandria (c.100–c.170 CE) built on the work of Hipparchus and others to produce his great work on astronomy, commonly known as the Almagest.

HIPPARCHUS

Although born in Nicaea in Bithynia, Hipparchus spent most of his life in Rhodes, where he built on the observations of earlier Greek astronomers and Babylonian records to produce a fine star catalog and set of planetary observations.

His use of these records and his own observations also led to what many claim as his finest achievement: his discovery of the precession of the equinoxes from a consideration of the slow motion of the points of the equinox and the solstice in the fixed stars. He also classified stars by their brightness, using a scale that ran from 1 (the brightest) to 6 (the dimmest).

Hipparchus incorporated data from his astronomical observations into his geometrical models used to explain astronomical motions.

Hipparchus is shown gazing at the stars, in an engraving from J. N. Larned's History of the World, *Vol. 1 (1897).*

He may also have developed an instrument of astrolabe type to derive the time at night from stellar observations.

SOME TRIGONOMETRY

Although little of Hipparchus's work survives, Claudius Ptolemy considered him his most important predecessor. Indeed, the subject of *trigonometry* (meaning angle-measuring), introduced by Hipparchus around 150 BCE, was developed by Claudius Ptolemy.

Fundamental to their work in astronomy was the calculation of the lengths of chords of circles—a chord is a line joining two points on the circle; it corresponds to working out the trigonometrical ratio called the sine for various angles.

The trigonometrical ratios arise from the study of right-angled triangles. If θ is the angle shown, we define the *sine*, *cosine*, and *tangent* of θ (written sin θ, cos θ, and tan θ) by the following ratios of lengths:

sin θ = opposite side / hypotenuse = a/c

cos θ = adjacent side / hypotenuse = b/c

tan θ = opposite side / adjacent side = a/b

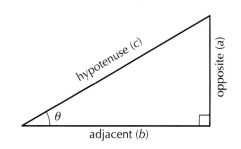

Ptolemy carries his cross-staff for measuring the heavens in this drawing by André Thevet, 1584.

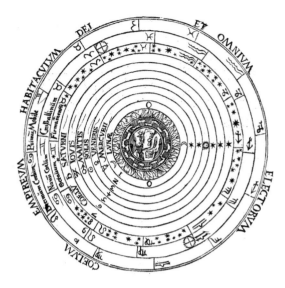

The Ptolemaic system, as portrayed in a Latin edition of the Almagest

To describe the motion of the sun and planets, Ptolemy introduced *epicycles*, small circles centered on the main circular orbit on which the sun or a planet is seen to move. Appropriately adjusting distances, the center of rotation, and the rates of rotations enabled him to make his accurate predictions.

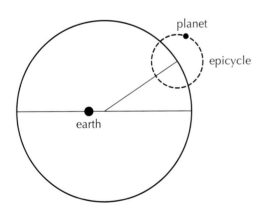

An epicycle in the Ptolemaic system

PTOLEMY'S *ALMAGEST*

Ptolemy's definitive thirteen-volume work on astronomy, the *Syntaxis*, is usually known by its later Arabic name *Almagest* (The Greatest). Dominating astronomy for nearly 1,500 years, it contains a mathematical description of the motion of the sun, moon, and planets, and has a table of chords equivalent to listing the sines of angles from 0° to 90° in steps of ¼°.

The *Almagest* is our most important source of information on Hipparchus, and we also know little of Ptolemy beyond what appears there.

Ptolemy's astronomical observations relate to the period 127–141 CE and were based at Alexandria; this is why he is often known as Claudius Ptolemy of Alexandria.

The *Almagest* developed a geometrical theory that could predict the motion of the planets to extraordinary accuracy. Ptolemy's geocentric cosmology regarded the earth as fixed and unmoving, with the sun and planets rotating around it.

Ptolemy's *Geographia*

Ptolemy also published a standard and influential work on map-making called *Geographia*, in which he discussed various types of map projection and listed the latitude and longitude of 8,000 places in the known world. His findings were used by navigators for over 1,500 years.

The Chinese

China's mathematical history dates back three thousand years or more. Around 220 BCE the ancient Chinese built the Great Wall, a major triumph of engineering skill and mathematical calculation. The Chinese may have been the first to develop a decimal place-value system, similar to the one we use today; they also constructed sundials and were early users of the abacus.

MAGIC SQUARES

An ancient Chinese legend concerns Emperor Yu of Xia, who was standing on the banks of the river Lo (a tributary of the Yellow River) when a sacred turtle emerged from the river with the numbers 1 to 9 on its back. These numbers appeared in the form of a 3 × 3 *magic square* (the *lo-shu*), an arrangement of numbers in which the numbers in each row, column, and diagonal have the same sum:

$$4 + 9 + 2 = 9 + 5 + 1 = 4 + 5 + 6 = 15, \text{ etc.}$$

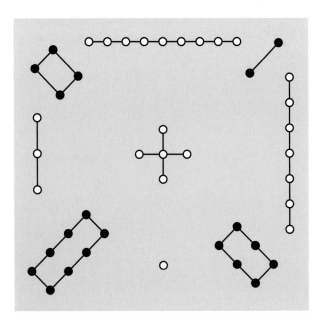

This particular arrangement of numbers acquired great religious and mystic significance over the centuries and appeared in many forms. Although Emperor Yu lived around 2000 BCE, no account of this story appeared until much later—possibly as late as the Han dynasty, which began in 206 BCE.

COUNTING

For their calculations the Chinese used a form of counting board, a box with separate compartments for units, tens, hundreds, etc., into which small bamboo rods were placed. Each symbol from 1 to 9 had two forms, horizontal and vertical, enabling the calculator to distinguish easily between the numbers in adjacent compartments. Here are the numbers 1713 and 6036.

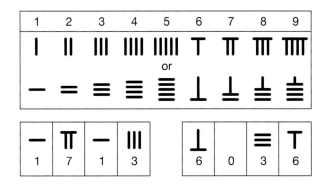

GOU-GU (PYTHAGOREAN THEOREM)

The Chinese used the idea of dissection (cutting up and reassembling) to obtain results in geometry. A celebrated example is *gou-gu*, their name for the Pythagorean theorem, which appears in the *Zhou bi suan jing* (Mathematical Classic of the Zhou Gnomon) from before 100 BCE. Our explanation below uses modern algebraic notation.

The diagram on page 29 shows a tilted square (of side c, say), surrounded by four right-angled triangles (with sides a, b, and c), making a large square (of side $a + b$). We now cut this large square of side $a + b$ into five pieces: the square of side c and the four triangles, each

Circle Measurement

Several Chinese mathematicians devoted their energies to estimating π.

Around the year 100 CE Zhang Heng, inventor of the seismograph for measuring the intensity of earthquakes, proposed the value $\sqrt{10}$ (about 3.16 in our decimal notation).

We saw how Archimedes calculated with regular polygons having 6, 12, 24, 48, and 96 sides to obtain the estimates $3^{10}/_{71} < π < 3^1/_7$ (about 3.14 in our decimal notation). In his *Haidao suanjing* (Sea Island Mathematical Classic) of 263, Liu Hui continued to double the number of sides until he reached polygons with 3,072 sides, obtaining the value π = 3.14159.

The Chinese fascination with π reached its climax in the fifth century, when Zu Chongzhi and his son calculated the areas of polygons with 24,576 sides and deduced that:

$$3.1415926 < π < 3.1415927$$

They also found the estimate of $3^{16}/_{113}$ (= $^{355}/_{113}$), which gives π to six decimal places: this approximation was not rediscovered in Europe until the sixteenth century.

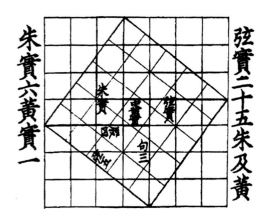

with area $\frac{1}{2}ab$. Then the area of the large square is $c^2 + (4 \times \frac{1}{2}ab) = c^2 + 2ab$ and is also:

$$(a + b)^2 = a^2 + b^2 + 2ab \text{—so } a^2 + b^2 = c^2$$

BAMBOO PROBLEM

A classic Chinese problem is the problem of the broken bamboo; a chi is a unit of length:

A bamboo 10 chi high is broken, and the upper end reaches the ground 3 chi from the stem. Find the height of the break.

In modern algebraic notation we can denote by x the height where the bamboo is broken, and by 10 – x the length of the rest of the bamboo.

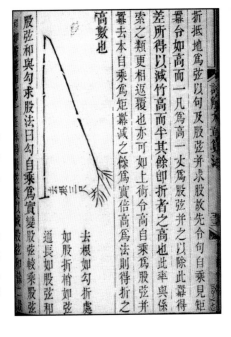

By the Pythagorean theorem:

$$x^2 + 3^2 = (10 - x)^2$$

Solving this equation gives $x = 4^{11}/_{20}$ chi.

THE NINE CHAPTERS

Most ancient Chinese mathematics was written on bamboo or paper, which perishes with time. One outstanding survivor, dating possibly from 200 BCE, is the *Jiu zhang suan shu* (Nine Chapters on the Mathematical Art).

This remarkable work contains 246 questions, with answers but no working shown, and may have been used as a textbook. It deals with both practical and theoretical matters—problems from trade, agriculture, surveying, and engineering, as well as discussions of the areas and volumes of various geometrical shapes, the calculation of square roots and cube roots, and the study of right-angled triangles. The *Nine Chapters* also includes a discussion of simultaneous equations using a method (now known as *Gaussian elimination*) that was not rediscovered in Europe until two thousand years later.

The Indians

Around 250 BCE King Asoka, ruler of most of India, became the first Buddhist monarch. His conversion was celebrated around the kingdom by the construction of many pillars carved with his edicts. These Asoka columns included the first known appearance of what would eventually become our Hindu–Arabic numerals, a decimal place-value system with separate columns for units, tens, hundreds, etc. From about the year 400 CE, the Indians also used the number 0, both as a place-holder and as a number to calculate with, and showed how to work with negative numbers.

Indian mathematics can be traced back to a number of Vedic manuscripts from around 600 BCE. These contain early work on arithmetic, permutations, and combinations, the theory of numbers, and the extraction of square roots.

Later, in the first millennium CE, the two most outstanding Indian mathematicians were Aryabhata the Elder (b. 476) and Brahmagupta (598–670).

ARYABHATA

One of Aryabhata's main contributions to mathematics was to arithmetic series: these are addition sums like:

$$5 + 9 + 13 + 17 + 21 + 25 + 29$$

India's Aryabhata satellite, 1975

where the difference between successive terms is always the same (in this case, 4). Aryabhata gave various rules for adding such numbers together, of which his simplest was:

Add the first and last terms and multiply the answer by half the number of terms.

For the series above, the sum of the first and last terms is $5 + 29 = 34$, and half the number of terms is $3\frac{1}{2}$; multiplying these together gives the correct answer, 119.

Aryabhata also presented (in words) formulas for the sum of the first few natural numbers and of their squares and cubes; in our modern notation these are:

$$1 + 2 + 3 + \ldots + n = n\,(n + 1)\,/2$$
$$1^2 + 2^2 + 3^2 + \ldots + n^2 = n\,(n + 1)\,(2n + 1)\,/6$$
$$1^3 + 2^3 + 3^3 + \ldots + n^3 = n^2\,(n + 1)^2\,/4$$

For example (with $n = 10$):

$$1 + 2 + \ldots + 10 = (10 \times 11)\,/2 = 55$$
$$1^2 + 2^2 + \ldots + 10^2 = (10 \times 11 \times 21)\,/6 = 385$$
$$1^3 + 2^3 + \ldots + 10^3 = (10^2 \times 11^2)\,/4 = 3{,}025$$

Aryabhata gave the first systematic treatment of Diophantine equations—algebraic problems for which we seek whole number solutions. He was also interested in trigonometry, constructed tables of the sine function, and obtained the value 3.1416 for π.

The first Indian satellite was named "Aryabhata" in his honor.

BRAHMAGUPTA

Indian mathematicians transformed zero from its role as a place-holder to an actual number to calculate with. In 628 CE, the astronomer and mathematician Brahmagupta completed a work called the *Brahmasphutasiddhanta* (The Opening of the Universe), in which he began with positive numbers or "fortunes" (such as 3), explained the use of zero (which he called both *cipher* and *nought*), and then extended his discussion to negative numbers or "debts" (such as S5)—a great breakthrough. He also gave explicit rules for combining them:

Brahmagupta

> *The sum of cipher and negative is negative; of positive and nought, positive; of two ciphers, cipher.*

[e.g., $0 + (-5) = -5$, $3 + 0 = 3$, $0 + 0 = 0$]

> *Negative taken from cipher becomes positive, and positive from cipher is negative; cipher taken from cipher is nought.*

[e.g., $0 - (-5) = 5$, $0 - 3 = -3$, $0 - 0 = 0$]

> *The product of cipher and positive, or of cipher and negative, is nought; of two ciphers is cipher…*

[e.g., $0 \times 3 = 0$, $0 \times (-5) = 0$, $0 \times 0 = 0$]

Brahmagupta also worked extensively on a particular type of Diophantine equation with two unknowns. It is now known as *Pell's equation*, after an incorrect assignation by the eighteenth-century mathematician Leonhard Euler. This equation has the form:

$$Cx^2 + 1 = y^2$$

and we are required to find whole number solutions for a given value of C. For example, when $C = 3$, we seek whole numbers x and y that satisfy the equation $3x^2 + 1 = y^2$. Two solutions are:

$x = 1$ and $y = 2$, since $(3 \times 1^2) + 1 = 4 = 2^2$

$x = 4$ and $y = 7$, since $(3 \times 4^2) + 1 = 49 = 7^2$

But if $x = 2$, then there is no value for y.

Brahmagupta solved Pell's equation for many different values of C, and also derived useful methods for generating new solutions from old; thus, if he could find a single solution to a particular equation, he could then find as many other solutions as he wished.

One particularly difficult case to crack was $61x^2 + 1 = y^2$ (with $C = 61$), where he found the simplest solution:

$x = 226,153,980$ and $y = 1,766,319,049$

A remarkable achievement. This solution was later rediscovered in the seventeenth century by the French mathematician Pierre de Fermat.

Cyclic Quadrilaterals

One of Brahmagupta's main interests was the study of quadrilaterals whose corners lie on a circle. He obtained formulas for the area of such a quadrilateral and for the lengths of the two diagonals, given the lengths of its four sides, and gave various methods for constructing such quadrilaterals.

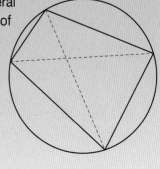

The Mayans

One of the most interesting counting systems is that of the Mayans of Central America, used between their most productive years from 300 to 1000 CE. The Mayans were situated over a large area centered on present-day Guatemala and Belize and extending from the Yucatan peninsula of Mexico in the north to Honduras in the south. Most of their calculations involved the construction of calendars, for which they developed a place-value system based mainly on the number 20.

Our knowledge of the Mayan counting system and of their calendars is derived mainly from writings on the walls of caves and ruins, hieroglyphic inscriptions on carved pillars (*stelae*), and a handful of painted manuscripts (*codices*). The codices were intended to guide Mayan priests in ritual ceremonies involving hunting, planting, and rainmaking, but many codices were destroyed by the Spanish conquerors who arrived in this area after the year 1500.

The most notable of the surviving codices is the beautiful *Dresden codex*, dating from about 1200. It is painted in color on a long strip of glazed fig-tree bark and contains many examples of Mayan numbers.

THE MAYAN NUMBER SYSTEM

The Mayan counting system was a place-value system with a dot to represent 1, a line to represent 5, and a special symbol (a shell) to represent 0. These were combined to give the numbers from 0 to 19.

To obtain larger numbers they combined these numbers, writing them vertically; for example,

the illustrated codex depicts the symbol for 12 above the symbol for 13—this represents the number 253 (12 twenties + 13).

THE MAYAN CALENDARS

In order to keep track of the passage of time, the Mayans employed two types of calendar, with 260 days and 365 days.

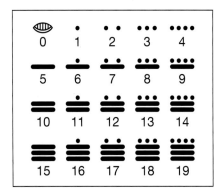

The Mayan symbols for the numbers from 0 to 19

32

Part of a Mayan codex

The 260-day calendar was a ritual one, used for forecasting and known as the *tzolkin*, or "sacred calendar." It consisted of thirteen months of twenty days. Each day combined a month-number (from 1 to 13) with one of twenty day-pictures named after deities (such as Imix, Ik, and Akbal). These two systems then intermeshed, as illustrated—for example, the day 1 Imix was not followed by 2 Imix and 3 Imix, but by 2 Ik and 3 Akbal, etc.—eventually yielding a cycle of 13 × 20 = 260 days.

For their 365-day calendar, they modified their number system to take account of the number of days in the calendar year. To do so, they introduced an 18 into their 20-based system (since 18 × 20 = 360), and then added five extra "inauspicious" days to make up the full 365 days. So their counting system was based on the following scheme:

1 kin = 1 day
20 kins = 1 uinal = 20 days
18 uinals = 1 tun = 360 days
20 tuns = 1 katun = 7,200 days
20 katuns = 1 baktun = 144,000 days

and so on. They had no problems in calculating with such large numbers.

These two calendars operated independently, and were also combined to give a *calendar round*, in which the number of days was the least common multiple of 260 and 365, which is 18,980 days, or 52 calendar years. These periods of 52 years were then packaged into even longer time periods. The longest time period used by the Mayans was the *long count* calendar of 5,125 years.

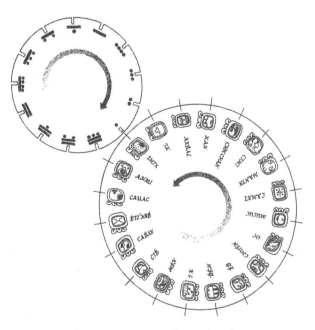

The Mayan 260-day calendar

al-Khwarizmi

The period from 750 to 1400 saw an awakening of interest in Greek and Indian culture in Mesopotamia. Inspired by the teachings of the prophet Muhammad, Islamic scholars seized on the ancient texts, translating them into Arabic and extending and commenting on them. Baghdad, on the trade routes for silk and spices, was well placed to receive the writings of Greek geometers and the contributions of Indian scholars—including the positional method of counting.

In Baghdad the caliphs actively promoted mathematics and astronomy, and in the early ninth century Caliph Harun al-Rashid and his son al-Ma'mun established and supported the "House of Wisdom," a scientific academy with its own extensive library and observatory. There, Islamic mathematicians translated and commented on the Greek works of Euclid, Archimedes, and others, and developed the Indian decimal place-value counting system into what are now the *Hindu–Arabic numerals*.

AL-KHWARIZMI (*c.*783–*c.*850)

One of the earliest scholars at the House of Wisdom was the Persian scholar Muhammad ibn-Musa (al-)Khwarizmi

(his Persian name omitted the Arabic prefix "al-"). The author of two celebrated astronomical star tables and an influential treatise on the astrolabe, he is remembered by mathematicians primarily for his books on arithmetic and algebra.

Neither book contained results of great originality, but his *Arithmetic* was important for introducing the Indian number system to the Islamic world and later helping to spread the decimal counting system throughout Christian Europe. Indeed, his Arabic name, transmuted into "algorism," was later used in Europe to mean arithmetic, and we still use the word *algorithm* to refer to a step-by-step procedure for solving problems.

The title of al-Khwarizmi's algebra book is *Kitab al-jabr wal-muqabala* (The Compendious Book on Calculation by Completion [*al-jabr*] and Reduction [*al-muqabala*]). This book title is the origin of our word "algebra": the term "al-jabr" refers to the operation of transposing a term from one side of an algebraic equation to the other.

A statue of al-Khwarizmi in Khiva, Uzbekistan

Solving a Quadratic Equation

One square, and ten roots of the same, amount to thirty-nine dirhems
(a dirhem is a unit of currency).

In modern notation, this is $x^2 + 10x = 39$.

To solve this, al-Khwarizmi started with a square of side x (shaded) and added two rectangles of length x and width 5 (note that 5 is half of 10). He then completed the square by adding a new square of side 5.

The resulting larger square of side $x + 5$ has area $(x + 5)^2$, and is made up from two smaller squares with areas x^2 and 25 and two rectangles each with area $5x$. Thus:

$$(x + 5)^2 = x^2 + 10x + 25$$

Since $x^2 + 10x = 39$, we have:

$$(x + 5)^2 = 39 + 25 = 64$$

Taking the square root, he found that $x + 5 = 8$, giving the solution $x = 3$.

Note that the other solution (–13), being a negative number, was not considered meaningful and was ignored.

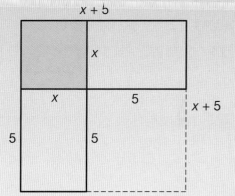

Al-Khwarizmi's *Algebra* commences with a lengthy account of how to solve linear equations (with numbers and terms involving x) and quadratic equations (also involving x^2). Since negative numbers were still not considered meaningful, he split the equations into the following six types, given here with their modern equivalents (where a, b, and c are positive constants):

roots equal to numbers ($ax = b$)

squares equal to numbers ($ax^2 = b$)

squares equal to roots ($ax^2 = bx$)

squares and roots equal to numbers
   ($ax^2 + bx = c$)

squares and numbers equal to roots
   ($ax^2 + c = bx$)

roots and numbers equal to squares
   ($bx + c = ax^2$)

He then proceeded to solve instances of each type, such as $x^2 + 10x = 39$ (see above), using a geometrical form of "completing the square."

Early Islamic astronomers using a theodolite, an instrument for measuring angles.

EARLY EUROPEAN MATHEMATICS

The revival of mathematical learning during the Middle Ages was largely due to three factors:

- *the translation of Arabic classical texts into Latin during the twelfth and thirteenth centuries;*
- *the establishment of the earliest European universities;*
- *the invention of printing.*

The first of these factors made the works of Euclid, Archimedes, and other Greek writers available to European scholars, the second enabled groups of like-minded scholars to meet and discourse on matters of common interest, while the last enabled scholarly works to be available at modest cost to the general populace in their own language.

The first European university was founded in Bologna in 1088, and Paris and Oxford followed shortly after. The curriculum was in two parts. The first part, studied for four years by those aspiring to a Bachelor's degree, was based on the ancient "trivium" of grammar, rhetoric, and logic (usually Aristotelian). The second part, leading to a Master's degree, was based on the "quadrivium," the Greek mathematical arts of arithmetic, geometry, astronomy, and music; the works studied included Euclid's *Elements* and Ptolemy's *Almagest*.

THE HINDU–ARABIC NUMERALS

We have seen how the decimal place-value system represented by the Hindu–Arabic numerals first arose in India and was later developed by al-Khwarizmi and other Islamic scholars working in Baghdad and elsewhere.

Gradually the numerals diverged into three separate types—the modern Hindu script, the East Arabic numerals (written from right to left) still found today in the countries of the Middle East, and the West Arabic numerals 1 to 9 and 0 (written from left to right) that eventually became the number system used throughout Western Europe.

However, it took many centuries for the Western form of the Hindu–Arabic numerals to become fully established. They were certainly proved more convenient to use for calculations than Roman numerals, but for practical use most people continued to use an abacus.

As time progressed the situation improved with the publication of influential books that promoted them, such as those by Fibonacci (in Latin), Pacioli (in Italian), and Recorde (in English). By the time that printed books had become widely available, Hindu–Arabic numerals were in general use.

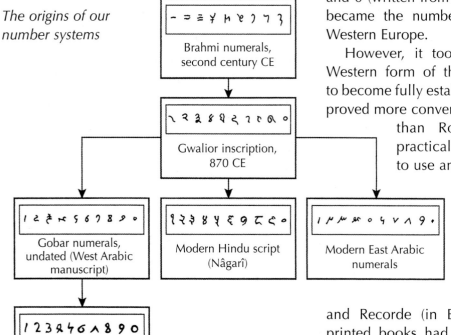

The origins of our number systems

Brahmi numerals, second century CE

Gwalior inscription, 870 CE

Gobar numerals, undated (West Arabic manuscript)

Modern Hindu script (Nâgarî)

Modern East Arabic numerals

Early printed numerals, 1474

THE AGE OF DISCOVERY

The spirit of enquiry and inventiveness of the Middle Ages and the Renaissance led people to adopt a more critical view of ideas that had been accepted for centuries. It showed itself in many ways:

- the voyages of discovery to unknown lands;

- the development and invention of scientific and mathematical instruments for a variety of purposes;

- the use of geometrical perspective in painting and other visual arts;

- the solution of cubic and quartic equations;

- the development and standardization of mathematical terminology and notation;

- the revolutionary approach to planetary motion;

- the rediscovery and reinterpretation of classical texts;

- the development of mechanics;

- the removal of algebra from its dependence on geometry.

These all contributed to the development of a view that the universe is a book written in the language of mathematics. As instruments became ever more sophisticated, mathematics for practical purposes increased—particularly in navigation, map-making, astronomy, and warfare.

Viewing the heavens with a joynt rule

37

Leonardo Fibonacci

Leonardo of Pisa (c.1170–1240), known since the nineteenth century as Fibonacci (son of Bonaccio), is remembered mainly for his Liber Abaci (Book of Calculation), which he used to popularize the Hindu–Arabic numerals, and for a number sequence named after him. His work was crucial in bringing Arabic mathematics to wider recognition in Western Europe.

Fibonacci was born in Pisa. After traveling widely throughout the Mediterranean, he returned home and wrote works expanding on what he had learned, to help his countrymen deal with calculation and commerce.

THE *LIBER ABACI*

Most of our knowledge about Fibonacci comes from the prologue of his influential book *Liber Abaci*. The first edition of this book appeared in 1202. It covers four main areas starting with the use of Hindu–Arabic numerals in calculation and then using them for the mathematics needed in business. The largest part of the book deals with recreational mathematical problems, finishing with operations on roots and a little geometry.

PROBLEMS FROM THE *LIBER ABACI*

Fibonacci's *Liber Abaci* contains a wide range of mathematical problems, including the following three that may be similar to ones you remember from your school days!

> *There is a tree, ¼ and ⅓ of which lie below ground. If the part below ground is 21 palmi, how tall is the tree?*

> *If a lion can eat a sheep in 4 hours, a leopard can eat it in 5 hours, and a bear can eat it in 6 hours, how long would they take eating it together?*

> *I can buy 3 sparrows for a cent, 2 turtle-doves for a cent, or doves for 2 cents each. If I spent 30 cents buying 30 birds and bought at least one bird of each kind, how many of each kind did I buy?*

Another problem involves adding powers of 7:

> *7 old women are going to Rome; each has 7 mules; each mule carries 7 sacks; each sack contains 7 loaves; each loaf has 7 knives; each knife has 7 sheaths; what is the total number of things?*

This is reminiscent of a problem from the Egyptian Rhind papyrus:

> *houses 7; cats 49; mice 343; spelt 2,401; hekat 16,807. Total 19,607.*

and of the more recent English nursery rhyme:

> *As I was going to St Ives I met a man with 7 wives … Kits, cats, sacks, and wives, How many were going to St Ives?*

Leonardo Fibonacci

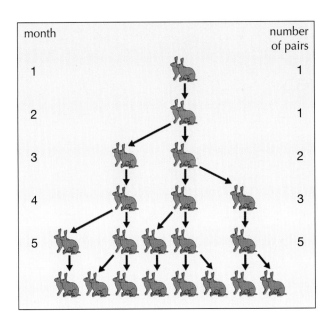

month	number of pairs
1	1
2	1
3	2
4	3
5	5

Such examples dramatically illustrate the fact that the same mathematical idea can resurface in different guises over thousands of years.

THE RABBITS PROBLEM

The most famous problem in the Liber Abaci is the problem of the rabbits:

> *A farmer has a pair of baby rabbits. Rabbits take two months to reach maturity and then give birth to another pair each month. How many pairs of rabbits are there after a year?*

To solve this, we note that:

- In months 1 and 2 the farmer has only the original pair,

- In month 3, a new pair arrives, so he now has two pairs,

- In month 4, the original pair produces another pair, and the new pair has not yet produced, so he now has three pairs,

- In month 5, the original pair and the new pair both produce another pair; and so on.

The result of the problem is that the number of rabbits in each month follows the so-called *Fibonacci* sequence:

1, 1, 2, 3, 5, 8, 13, 21, 34, 55, 89, 144, ...,

in which each successive number (after the first two) is the sum of the previous two; for example, 89 = 34 + 55. The answer to the problem is the twelfth number, which is 144.

SPIRALS AND THE GOLDEN NUMBER

The ratios of successive terms of the Fibonacci sequence are:

$$\frac{1}{1}, \frac{2}{1}, \frac{3}{2}, \frac{5}{3}, \frac{8}{5}, ...$$

These tend to the "golden number"

$$\varphi = \frac{1}{2}(1 + \sqrt{5}) = 1.618...$$

which has remarkable and pleasing properties: for example, to find its square we add 1 ($\varphi^2 = 2.618...$), and to find its reciprocal we subtract 1 ($1/\varphi = 0.618...$).

A rectangle whose sides are in the ratio φ to 1 is often considered to have the most pleasing shape—neither too thin, nor too fat. The following picture shows how the Fibonacci numbers can be arranged so as to give rise to a spiral pattern; further rectangles can be added at will.

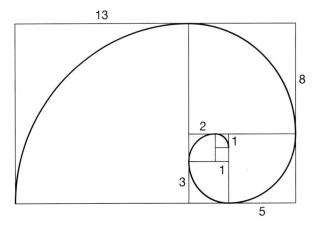

Similar spirals occur through nature—on a nautilus shell and in the pattern of seeds in a sunflower—for example, the number of seeds in such a spiral pattern is often 34, 55, or 89, all of which are Fibonacci numbers.

Robert Recorde

In England the earliest published books with any mathematical content were in Latin. These included Cuthbert Tunstall's De Arte Supputandi (On the Art of Reckoning) of 1522, the first arithmetic text published in England, and the best of its time. But gradually, vernacular works in English began to appear.

The first arithmetic book to be published in English may have been a work from St Albans in 1537 entitled *An Introduction for to Lerne to Reken with the Pen and with the Counters, after the Trewe Cast of Arismetyke or Awgrym in Hole Numbers, and also in Broken* (the word *awgrym* means mathematics, and *broken* numbers are fractions). But the most important early writer of mathematical textbooks in English was Robert Recorde (1510–58).

RECORDE'S LIFE

Recorde had an eventful life. Graduating from Oxford University in 1531, he was elected a Fellow of All Souls, before going to Cambridge to study mathematics and medicine. Later he became General Surveyor of the Mines and Monies in Ireland, until the project was closed down. He then apparently went to London, acting as physician to Edward VI and Queen Mary. When his rival, the Earl of Pembroke, led troops to dispel a rebellion against the queen, Recorde tried to charge him with misconduct and was sued for libel. Unable or unwilling to pay his fine, he was thrown into a London jail for debt and died there.

On the educational side, Recorde was a highly respected communicator. His books, all written in English, were designed to teach mathematics and its applications to the general reader and ran to many editions. Most of them were written in the form of a Socratic dialogue between a Scholar and his Master.

THE GROUND OF ARTES (1543)

The first of Recorde's books, *The Ground of Artes*, was an arithmetic text teaching "the Worke and Practise, of Arithmeticke, both in whole numbers and fractions" and explaining the various rules so simply that "euerie child can do it." In addition to leading the Scholar through the techniques that he needed to learn, the Master explained the importance of arithmetic in everyday life, discussed its uses in commerce and war, and justified its appearance in such "other Sciences, as Musick, Physick, Law, Grammer, and such like." However, the Master's advice was occasionally less than encouraging:

Scholar. *Syr, what is the chiefe use of Multiplication?*
Mayster. *The use of it is greater than you can yet understand.*

In this section on multiplication the Master explained how to carry out multiplication sums. To multiply 8 by 7, for

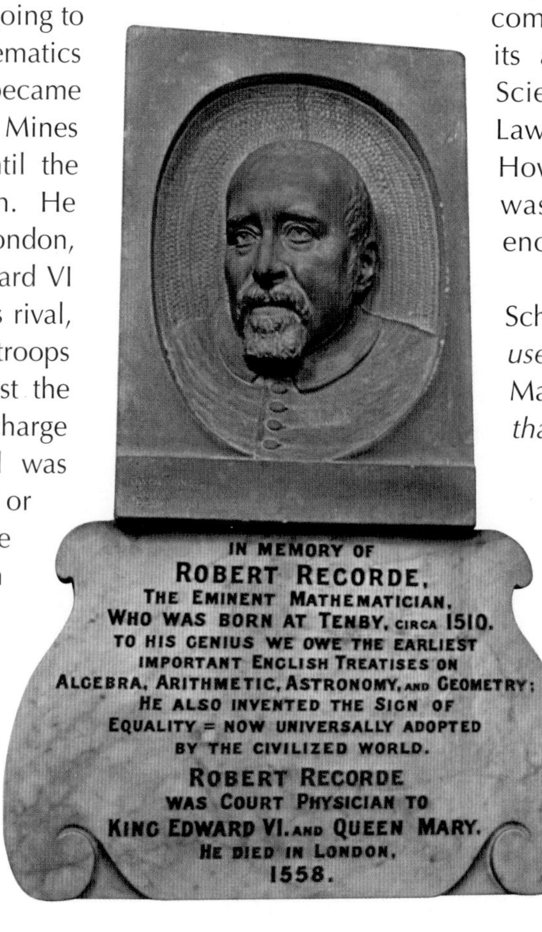

IN MEMORY OF
ROBERT RECORDE,
THE EMINENT MATHEMATICIAN,
WHO WAS BORN AT TENBY, CIRCA 1510.
TO HIS GENIUS WE OWE THE EARLIEST
IMPORTANT ENGLISH TREATISES ON
ALGEBRA, ARITHMETIC, ASTRONOMY, AND GEOMETRY;
HE ALSO INVENTED THE SIGN OF
EQUALITY = NOW UNIVERSALLY ADOPTED
BY THE CIVILIZED WORLD.
ROBERT RECORDE
WAS COURT PHYSICIAN TO
KING EDWARD VI. AND QUEEN MARY,
HE DIED IN LONDON,
1558.

A memorial to Robert Recorde in St Mary's Church, Tenby, South Wales

example, he wrote these numbers on the left, and opposite he subtracted each from 10, giving 2 and 3.

Now 8 − 3 (or 7 − 2) = 5, and 3 × 2 = 6, so the answer is 56.

The cross eventually shrank in size and became the multiplication sign that we use today.

THE PATHWAY TO KNOWLEDGE (1551)

The appearance of printed books led to standardization in terminology. In his geometry text, *The Pathway to Knowledge*, Recorde introduced the term *straight line*, which is still used. He also proposed several attractive terms that never caught on, such as *prickes* for points,

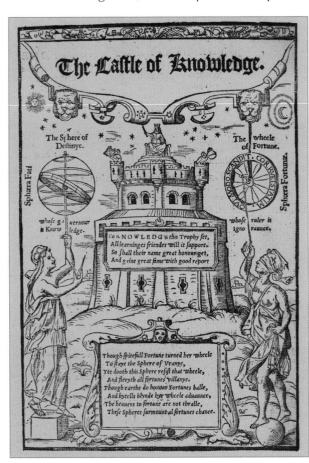

Recorde's The Castle of Knowledge

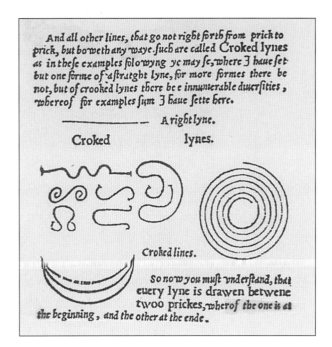

And all other lines, that go not right forth from prick to prick, but boweth any waye. such are called Croked lynes as in these examples folowyng ye may se, where I haue set but one forme of a straight line, for more formes there be not, but of crooked lynes there be e innumerable diuersities, whereof for examples sum I haue sette here.

——————— A right lyne.

Croked lynes.

Croked lines.

So now you must vnderstand, that euery lyne is drawen betwene twoo prickes, wherof the one is at the beginning, and the other at the ende.

An extract from The Pathway to Knowledge

sharp and *blunt corners* for acute and obtuse angles, a *touch line* for a tangent, *threelike* for an equilateral triangle, and a *likejamme* for a parallelogram.

THE WHETSTONE OF WITTE (1557)

Recorde's most celebrated use of new notation made its first appearance in *The Whetstone of Witte*, his textbook on algebra. In this work he explains that,

> to avoide the tediouse repetition of these woordes: is equalle to: I will sette as I doe often in woorde use, a paire of paralleles, o: Gemowe lines of one lengthe, thus: ======, bicause noe.2. thynges, can be moare equalle.

This was the first appearance of our equals sign; it was much longer than our current version.

1. $14.\textit{ze}. +.15.\textit{9} ===== 71.\textit{9}.$
2. $20.\textit{ze}. ———.18.\textit{9} ===.102.\textit{9}.$
3. $26.\textit{z}. + 10\textit{ze} == 9.\textit{z}.— 10\textit{ze} + 213.\textit{9}.$

Recorde's other books included a book on medicine called *The Urinal of Physick* (1548) and an astronomy text entitled *The Castle of Knowledge* (1556).

Cardano and Tartaglia

The attempt to solve cubic equations is one of the most celebrated stories in the history of mathematics. It took place in Bologna in the early sixteenth century, during a period when Italian university academics had little job security. Having to compete annually for their positions, they often had to prove their superiority over their rivals by resorting to public problem-solving contests.

In the eleventh century, Omar Khayyám classified cubic equations and solved one by intersecting a semicircle with a parabola; but little further progress was made on solving cubic equations in general, and even around 1500 Pacioli and others were pessimistic as to whether this could be done.

However, in the 1520s, Scipione del Ferro, a mathematics lecturer at the University of Bologna, found a general method for solving cubic equations of the form:

A cube and things equal to numbers

(which we would write as $x^3 + cx = d$), and revealed it to his pupil Antonio Fior.

Another who investigated cubic equations around this time was Niccolò of Brescia (1499/1500–1557), known as Tartaglia ("the stammerer")

Niccolò Tartaglia

from a bad stammer that he developed after being slashed by a saber across the face as a boy. In particular, Tartaglia found a method for solving equations of the form:

A cube and squares equal to numbers

(which we would write as $x^3 + bx^2 = d$).

FIOR CHALLENGES TARTAGLIA

After del Ferro's death in 1526, Fior felt free to exploit his secret, and challenged Tartaglia to a cubic-solving contest. Fior presented him with thirty cubic equations of the first form, giving him a month to solve them. Tartaglia in turn presented Fior with thirty cubic equations of the second form.

Here are two of Fior's problems, with their modern equivalents:

Find me a number such that when its cube root is added to it, the result is 6. [$x^3 + x = 6$]

A man sells a sapphire for 500 ducats, making a profit of the cube root of his capital. How much is this profit? [$x^3 + x = 500$]

Fior lost the contest. He was not a good enough mathematician to solve Tartaglia's type of problem, while Tartaglia, during a sleepless night ten days before the contest, managed to discover a method for solving all of Fior's problems.

GEROLAMO CARDANO

Meanwhile in Milan, Gerolamo Cardano (1501–76) was writing extensively about a range of topics, from physics and medicine to algebra

Tartaglia's Method for Solving $x^3 + cx = d$

In order to keep it secret, Tartaglia memorized his method in the form of a verse. This appears in italics below, together with the general method and a solution in a particular case—the equation:

$x3 + 18x = 19$, where $c = 18$ and $d = 19$

The method involves finding two numbers u and v satisfying $u - v = d$ and $uv = (c/3)^3$ and then writing $x = 3\sqrt{u} - 3\sqrt{v}$.

When the cube and the thing together:
Are equal to some discrete number, $[x^3 + cx = d:$ $x^3 + 18x = 19]$
Find two other numbers differing in this one. $[u - v = d:$ $u - v = 19]$
Then you will keep this as a habit
That their product shall always be equal
Exactly to the cube of a third of the things. $[uv = (c/3)^3:$ $uv = 6^3 = 216]$
The remainder then as a general rule $[$Find $u, v:$ $u = 27, v = 8]$
Of their cube roots subtracted $[$Find $^3\sqrt{u}, ^3\sqrt{v}:$ $^3\sqrt{u} = 3, ^3\sqrt{v} = 2]$
Will be equal to this principal thing. $[x = ^3\sqrt{u} - ^3\sqrt{v}:$ $x = 3 - 2 = 1$, so $x = 1]$

and probability (especially its applications to gambling). On hearing about the contest, Cardano determined to prise Tartaglia's method out of him.

This he did one evening in 1539, after promising Tartaglia an introduction to the Spanish governor of the city. Tartaglia hoped that the governor would fund his researches, and in turn extracted from Cardano the following solemn oath not to reveal his method of solution:

I swear to you, by God's holy Gospels, and as a true man of honor, not only never to publish your discoveries, if you teach me them, but I also promise you, and I pledge my faith as a true Christian, to note them down in code, so that after my death, no one will be able to understand them.

However, in 1542 Cardano learned that the original discovery of Tartaglia's method had been due to del Ferro, and he felt free to break his oath. Meanwhile, his brilliant colleague Ludovico Ferrari had found a similar general method for solving quartic equations (involving terms in x4).

In 1545, Cardano published *Ars Magna* (The Great Art), containing the methods for solving cubics and quartics and giving credit to Tartaglia. The *Ars Magna* became one of the most

important algebra books of all time, but Tartaglia was outraged by Cardano's behavior and spent the rest of his life writing him vitriolic letters.

Thus, after a struggle lasting many centuries, cubic equations had at last been solved, together with quartic equations. The next question (*Can one solve equations involving x^5, x^6,…?*) remained open until the nineteenth century.

Gerolamo Cardano

Rafael Bombelli

For most purposes our ordinary number system is all we need. In this system we can take the square root of numbers such as 3, √2 and π, but not the square root of the negative number −1: this is because both positive and negative numbers have positive squares, so what number can one square to give −1? Cardano and Bombelli came across this problem while trying to solve quadratic and cubic equations, and they found it useful to calculate with the mysterious object √−1, even though they did not understand what it was.

One numerical problem that Cardano tried to solve was:

Divide 10 into two parts whose product is 40

On taking the parts to be x and $10 − x$, he obtained the quadratic equation:

Title page of Bombelli's *Algebra*

$$x (10 − x) = 40$$

Solving this, he obtained the solutions $5 + \sqrt{-15}$ and $5 − \sqrt{-15}$. He could see no meaning to these, but observed:

Nevertheless we will operate, putting aside the mental tortures involved…

and found that everything worked out correctly:

- the sum is $(5 + \sqrt{-15}) + (5 − \sqrt{-15}) = 10$;
- the product is $(5 + \sqrt{-15}) \times (5 − \sqrt{-15})$ $= 5^2 − (\sqrt{-15})^2 = 25 − (−15) = 40$.

In view of these "mental tortures," Cardano was led to complain that:

So progresses arithmetic subtlety, the end of which is as refined as it is useless.

BOMBELLI'S EQUATIONS

The situation was greatly clarified by Rafael Bombelli (*c.*1526–72), who was born in Bologna and later worked as an engineer, draining swampy marshes and reclaiming them for the Catholic Church.

Growing up in Bologna, Bombelli was aware of the dispute between Cardano and Tartaglia and became interested in cubic equations and how to solve them. In particular, he considered the equation $x^3 = 15x + 4$, which has three real solutions:

$$x = 4, \; -2 + \sqrt{3} \;\text{ and }\; -2 - \sqrt{3}$$

with not an imaginary number in sight. However, on applying Tartaglia's method to solve this cubic equation, Bombelli was surprised to obtain the solution:

$$x = \sqrt[3]{(2 + \sqrt{-121})} + \sqrt[3]{(2 - \sqrt{-121})}$$

which involves complex numbers.

To explain the connection between his solution and the solution $x = 4$, Bombelli looked for real numbers a and b such that:

$$(a + b\sqrt{-1})^3 = 2 + \sqrt{-121}$$
$$\text{and } (a - b\sqrt{-1})^3 = 2 - \sqrt{-121}$$

so that he could take the two cube roots. After some experimentation, he found that $a = 2$ and $b = 1$:

$$(2 + \sqrt{-1})^3 = 2 + \sqrt{-121}$$
$$\text{and } (2 - \sqrt{-1})^3 = 2 - \sqrt{-121}$$

And so $x = (2 + \sqrt{-1}) + (2 - \sqrt{-1}) = 4$, as expected.

BOMBELLI'S *ALGEBRA*

Throughout his life Bombelli studied the algebraic writings of his predecessors, such as al-Khwarizmi, Fibonacci, and Pacioli. He also embarked on a major study of the works of Diophantus, having been shown a copy of the *Arithmetica* in a library in Rome.

Believing that no one had really explained clearly the nature of algebraic problems, and of how to solve cubic equations in particular, Bombelli embarked on a major project in which he proposed to present all that was known about the subject in an accessible form. Although five volumes of his *Algebra* were planned, only three were completed before his death. Incomplete manuscripts of the final two volumes (the "geometrical part") were discovered in a Bologna library in 1923.

In his *Algebra* Bombelli described how he had struggled hard to understand complex numbers. He was the first to show how to add and subtract them, and he gave rules for multiplying them. Using these rules, Bombelli showed how to obtain real solutions of cubic equations, even when Tartaglia's method yields square roots of negative numbers.

Complex Numbers

Suppose we try to calculate with the symbol $\sqrt{-1}$. We find that addition is easy:

$$(2 + 3\sqrt{-1}) + (4 + 5\sqrt{-1}) = 6 + 8\sqrt{-1}$$

and so is multiplication (replacing $\sqrt{-1} \times \sqrt{-1}$ whenever it appears by -1):

$$(2 + 3\sqrt{-1}) \times (4 + 5\sqrt{-1}) = (2 \times 4) + (3\sqrt{-1} \times 4) + (2 \times 5\sqrt{-1}) + (15 \times \sqrt{-1} \times \sqrt{-1})$$
$$= (8 - 15) + (12 + 10)\sqrt{-1} = -7 + 22\sqrt{-1}$$

We can carry out all the standard operations of arithmetic on these new objects. We call the object $a + b\sqrt{-1}$ a *complex number*: the number a is its *real part*, and the number b is its imaginary part. Nowadays, we usually use the letter i to mean $\sqrt{-1}$, so that $i^2 = -1$.

In 1799 complex numbers were given a geometrical form by the Danish navigator Caspar Wessel. In this representation, called the complex plane, two axes are drawn at right angles (the real axis and the imaginary axis) and the complex number $a + b\sqrt{-1}$ is represented by the point at distance a in the direction of the real axis and height b in the direction of the imaginary axis.

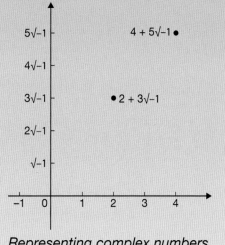

Representing complex numbers

Copernicus and Galileo

Nicolaus Copernicus (1473–1543), the "Father of Modern Astronomy," was born in Torun in Poland, and studied in Cracow, Bologna, and Ferrara. He transformed his subject by replacing Ptolemy's earth-centered system of planetary motion by a heliocentric system with the sun at the center and the earth as just one of several planets traveling in circular orbits around it. In 1632, Galileo Galilei (1564–1642), the "Father of Modern Physical Science," described the advantages of the Copernican system over Ptolemy's, bringing him into trouble with the Inquisition. In 1638 he wrote a book on mechanics that set the scene for the work of Isaac Newton and others.

NICOLAUS COPERNICUS

Although the heliocentric idea had been suggested earlier by Aristarchus and others, Copernicus was the first to work out the underlying theory and its consequences in mathematical detail.

His book *De Revolutionibus Orbium Coelestium* (On the Revolutions of the Heavenly Spheres) was published in 1543 and a copy was reportedly presented to him as he lay on his deathbed. In this celebrated work, he showed that the six planets then known split into two groups: Mercury and Venus (with orbits inside that of Earth), and Mars, Jupiter, and Saturn (with orbits outside it). He listed these planets

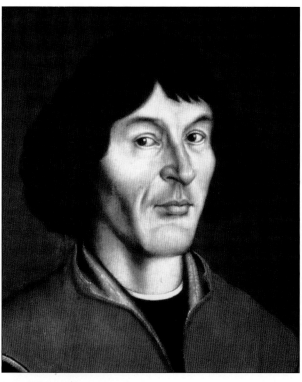

Nicolaus Copernicus

in increasing order of distance from the sun, and thereby illuminated phenomena that the Ptolemaic system had failed to explain, such as why Mercury and Venus are visible only at dawn and dusk while the other planets are visible throughout the night.

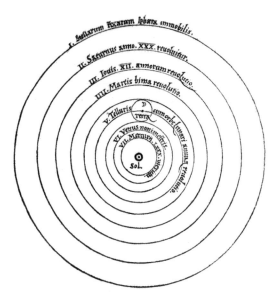

Copernicus's heliocentric system, from De Revolutionibus Orbium Coelestium

GALILEO GALILEI

The Copernican solar system aroused much controversy and brought its supporters into direct conflict with the Church, who considered

of the Copernican system. In the Ptolemaic system the same amount of Venus would always be visible, whereas in the Copernican system it should show phases (different amounts visible at different times). He turned his telescope on Venus and over the following few nights observed its phases.

Galileo's *Two Chief World Systems* was written in Italian and takes the form of a discussion over four days between two philosophers and a layman. They are Salviati who argues for the Copernican position and presents Galileo's views, Sagredo, the layman, who is seeking the truth and Simplicio, a follower of Aristotle and Ptolemy, who presents the traditional views and arguments.

Left: *Frontispiece of the* Two Chief World Systems, *depicting Aristotle, Ptolemy, and Copernicus in animated conversation*

the earth to lie at the center of Creation, so that Copernicus's ideas were at variance with the Holy Scriptures. It was Galileo who gave the most compelling exposition of the Copernican theory in his *Dialogo sopra I Due Massimi Sistemi del Mondo* (Dialogue Concerning the Two Chief World Systems) (1632). This led to his trial by the Inquisition, when he was forced to recant his Copernican views. He was not pardoned by the Church until 1995.

Galileo was born in Pisa and taught mathematics in Padua from 1592 to 1610, after which he became mathematician and philosopher to the Grand Duke at Florence. He was one of the first astronomers to make extensive use of the telescope, discovering sunspots and the moons of Jupiter and drawing the moon's surface. This instrument also enabled him to obtain observational evidence in favor

Galileo's Mechanics

In his mechanics book of 1638, Galileo discussed the laws of uniform and accelerated motion and explained why the path of a projectile must be a parabola.

In this book he gathered together a lifetime of study, presenting a theory of how position, velocity, and acceleration vary with time and supporting it with mathematical deductions. It was here that he laid the mathematical foundations underpinning his belief that the earth really moves. Its mathematical form laid a foundation for further advance by others, and particularly by Isaac Newton who was born in the year that Galileo died.

Johannes Kepler

Johannes Kepler (1571–1630) was born in Swabia in southwest Germany. A gifted and well-read mathematician in the Neoplatonist tradition, he based his work on harmony and design. A powerful early expression of this was his model of the solar system, and subsequently the three planetary laws that bear his name. Kepler also investigated polyhedra and contributed to what became the integral calculus.

The Danish astronomer Tycho Brahe (1546–1601) was the greatest observer of the heavens before the invention of the telescope, working for many years at his observatory of Uraniborg on the Danish island of Hven, before moving to Prague. Kepler became his assistant in Prague and in 1601 was appointed Imperial Mathematician to succeed Brahe after Brahe's untimely death. Kepler spent the next eleven years in Prague and produced some of his most important work there.

Kepler's Calculus

Kepler was interested in what was later known as the *integral calculus*, in which areas and volumes of geometrical shapes are calculated.

To obtain such areas and volumes he used what came to be called "the method of infinitesimals." By dividing a volume into very thin discs, for example, he determined the volumes of over ninety solids obtained by rotating conics and other curves around an axis.

KEPLER'S LAWS OF PLANETARY MOTION

What was needed to support the Copernican theory was a method of calculating heavenly events with at least as much accuracy as the Ptolemaic theory had done with its apparatus of epicycles. Using Brahe's extensive observational records, Kepler was eventually led, in his *Astronomia Nova* (The New Astronomy) (1609) and *Harmonices Mundi* (Harmony of the World) (1619), to the three laws that enabled him to make these calculations:

1. *The planets move in elliptical orbits with the sun at one focus.*

2. *The line from the sun to a planet sweeps out equal areas in equal times.*

3. *The square of a planet's period is proportional to the cube of its orbit's mean radius.*

Johannes Kepler

The following diagram illustrates Kepler's first and second laws. It shows a planet in elliptical orbit around the sun which is at a focus of the ellipse, and depicts the path traveled by the planet during three equal periods in its orbit. Kepler's second law tells us that these shaded areas are equal.

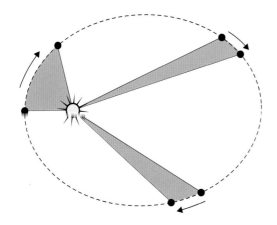

Kepler's laws were based on observed results; it was to be Newton, some eighty years later in his *Principia Mathematica*, who explained why they are true.

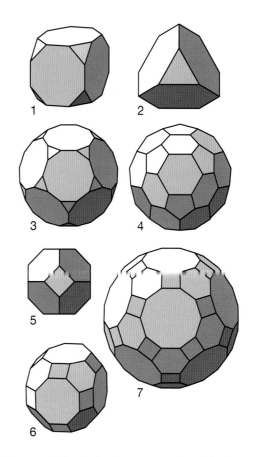

Some of Kepler's drawings of polyhedra

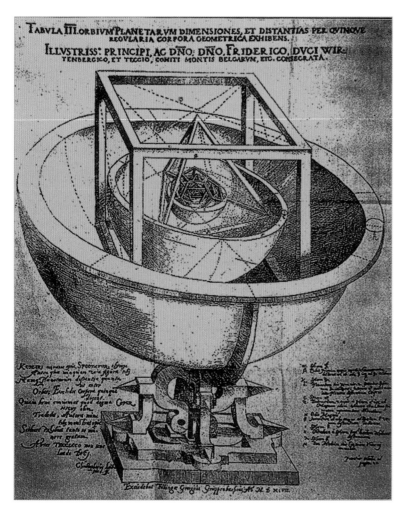

MATHEMATICAL PURSUITS

In his *Mysterium Cosmographicum* (The Cosmographic Mystery) of 1596, Kepler proposed a model of the solar system in which the five Platonic solids were set inside each other (with the octahedron innermost, followed by the icosahedron, dodecahedron, tetrahedron, and cube) and then interspersed with six spheres that carried the orbits of the then-known planets (Mercury, Venus, Earth, Mars, Jupiter, and Saturn).

Kepler was also interested in polyhedra in general, discovering the cuboctahedron and the antiprisms, and his name is associated with the four *Kepler–Poinsot star polyhedra*.

Left: *Kepler's model of the solar system*

AWAKENING AND ENLIGHTENMENT

The seventeenth and eighteenth centuries witnessed the beginnings of modern mathematics. New areas of the subject came into being—notably, analytic geometry and the calculus—while others, such as number theory, were reborn or took on a new lease of life. Fundamental problems, such as that of determining the orbits of the heavenly bodies, were solved or investigated with novel techniques.

It was the age of Newton in England, Descartes and Pascal in France, and Leibniz in Germany, followed by a succession of Continental "greats": the Bernoulli brothers, Euler, Lagrange, and Laplace.

It was also the age of gatherings—the formation of national scientific societies, such as London's Royal Society and the Academy of Sciences in Paris, and the founding of scholarly institutions such as the St Petersburg Academy and the Academy of Sciences in Berlin.

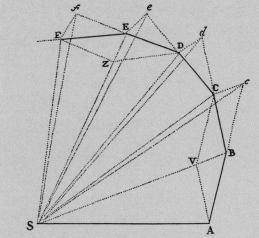

> ## PROPOSITION I. THEOREM I
> *The areas which revolving bodies describe by radii drawn to an immovable centre of force do lie in the same immovable planes, and are proportional to the times in which they are described.*
>
> For suppose the time to be divided into equal parts, and in the first part of that time let the body by its innate force describe the right line AB. In the second part of that time, the same would (by Law I), if not hindered,
>
> proceed directly to *c*, along the line B*c* equal to AB; so that by the radii AS, BS, *c*S, drawn to the centre, the equal areas ASB, BS*c*, would be described. But when the body is arrived at B, suppose that a centripetal force acts at once with a great impulse, and, turning aside the body from the right line B*c*, compels it afterwards to continue its motion along the right line BC.

The area swept out by a moving body: Newton's use of geometry (above) contrasts with Laplace's analytical approach (right).

CALCULUS AND DISCOVERY

Initially, the problems that mathematicians solved were geometrical, as were their answers, although the techniques they used (including the calculus) were not necessarily of this kind, being seen as methods of proceeding from a geometrical problem to a geometrical answer. The eighteenth century then led to a new conception of mathematics, with its most striking characteristic being its algebraic appearance.

The objects of mathematics were now described by formulas with symbols for variables and constants. A main reason for doing so was that the machinery of the calculus could then be applied both to them and to practical situations. This hastened the development of new

> If we project the body m, on the plane of x and y, the differential $(xdy - ydx)/2$, will represent the area which the radius vector, drawn from the origin of the coordinates to the projection of m, describes in the time dt, consequently the sum of the areas, multiplied respectively by the masses of the bodies, is proportional to the element of time, from which it follows that in a finite time, it is proportional to the time. It is this that constitutes the principle of the conservation of areas.

What is the Calculus?

The calculus is made up from two seemingly unrelated strands, now called *differentiation* and *integration*. Differentiation is concerned with how fast things move or change, and is used in the finding of velocities and tangents to curves. Integration is used to find areas of shapes in two-dimensional space or volumes in three dimensions.

As the seventeenth century progressed, it was gradually realized that these two strands are intimately related. As both Newton and Leibniz explained, they are inverse processes—if we follow either by the other, we return to our starting point.

However, Newton and Leibniz had different motivations, with Newton focusing on motion and Leibniz concerned with tangents and areas.

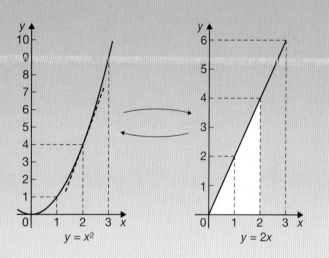

$y = x^2$

$y = 2x$

mathematical descriptions and techniques, such as in the emerging area of *differential equations*.

This shift toward the algebraic type of description also led to a good way of discovering new objects. Books were written in the algebraic style, and mathematicians formulated, thought about, and solved problems in this way. Algebra increasingly came to be seen as a logical language suitable for the investigation of all the sciences.

Mechanics and astronomy were the main areas of practical investigation. They both applied the calculus to functions of more than one variable, such as:

$$u(x, y) = x^6 + x^2y^2 + y^4$$

Here, $u(x, y)$ can be thought of as the height of a surface above the point with coordinates (x, y) in the plane.

The equations that arose were called *partial differential equations*, because they involved "partial differentiation." The partial derivative $\partial u/\partial x$ is the rate of change of u in the x-direction, while the partial derivative $\partial u/\partial y$ is the rate of change of u in the y-direction.

Louis XIV visits the Paris Academy of Sciences, 1671.

Napier and Briggs

In 1614 John Napier (1550–1617), 8th Laird of Merchiston (near Edinburgh), introduced logarithms as an aid to mathematical calculation, designed to replace lengthy computations involving multiplications and divisions by simpler ones using additions and subtractions. Being awkward to use, they were soon supplanted by others due to Henry Briggs (1561–1630), and their use proved an enormous boon to navigators and astronomers.

Early ideas of logarithms had appeared around the year 1500. Nicolas Chuquet and Michael Stifel listed the first few powers of 2 and noticed that to multiply two of them one simply adds their exponents—so, to multiply 16 and 128 we calculate:

$16 \times 128 = 2^4 \times 2^7 = 2^{4+7} = 2^{11} = 2048$,
and write $\log_2 2048 = 11$

NAPIER'S LOGARITHMS

The idea was not developed until Napier produced his *Mirifici Logarithmorum Canonis Descriptio* (A Description of the Admirable Table of Logarithms). This contains extensive tables

John Napier

The title page of Napier's logarithms

of logarithms of the sines and tangents of all the angles from 0 to 90 degrees, in steps of 1 minute; Napier's use of these logarithms arose because he intended them to be used as an aid to calculation by navigators and astronomers.

Napier's logarithms are not the ones we use now. He then considered two points moving along straight lines. The first travels at constant speed for ever, while the second, representing its logarithm, moves from *P* along a finite line *PQ* in such a way that its speed at each point is proportional to the distance it still has to travel.

In order to avoid the use of fractions he multiplied all his numbers by ten million.

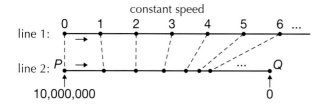

It follows from Napier's definition that the logarithm of 10,000,000 is 0. It can also be shown that, with his definition:

$$\log ab = \log a + \log b - \log 1$$

for any numbers a and b; here, log 1 has the cumbersome value of 161,180,956, which has to be subtracted in any calculation.

Napier also constructed from ivory a set of rods with numbers marked on them (now called *Napier's bones or rods*), which could be used to multiply numbers mechanically.

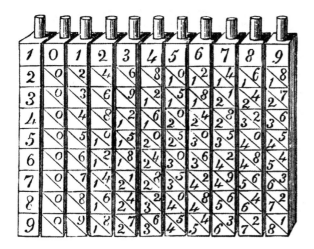

Napier's rods

HENRY BRIGGS

Shortly after their invention, Henry Briggs, first Gresham Professor of Geometry in London, heard about logarithms and enthused:

> *[John Napier] set my Head and hands a Work with his new and remarkable logarithms.*
>
> *I never saw a Book which pleased me better or made me more wonder.*

Briggs realized that Napier's logarithms were cumbersome, and felt that they could be redefined so as to avoid having to subtract the term log 1:

> *I myself, when expounding this doctrine to my auditors in Gresham College, remarked that it would be much more convenient that 0 should be kept for the logarithm of the whole sine.*

A related difficulty was that multiplication by 10 involved the addition of log 10 = 23,025,842.

Briggs twice visited Edinburgh to stay with Napier and sort out the difficulties. On returning to London, he devised a new form of logarithms, his logs to base 10, written $\log_{10}$, in which $\log_{10}$ 1 = 0 and $\log_{10}$ 10 = 1: to multiply two numbers one then simply adds their logarithms:

$$\log_{10} ab = \log_{10} a + \log_{10} b$$

in general, if $y = 10^x$, then $\log_{10} y = x$. In 1617 he published these in a small printed pamphlet, *Logarithmorum Chilias Prima* (The First Thousand Logarithms).

In 1624, after he had left London to become the first Savilian Professor of Geometry in Oxford, Briggs produced an extensive collection of logarithms to base 10 of the integers from 1 to 20,000 and 90,000 to 100,000, all calculated by hand to fourteen decimal places. The gap in his tables (from 20,000 to 90,000) was soon filled by the Dutch mathematician Adriaan Vlacq in 1628.

The invention of logarithms quickly led to the development of mathematical instruments based on a logarithmic scale. Most notable among these was the *slide rule*, versions of which first appeared around 1630 and were widely used for over three hundred years until the advent of the pocket calculator in the 1970s.

℀	*Logarithmi.*			*Logarithmi.*
1	00000,00000,00000	34	15314,78917,04226
2	03010,29995,66398	35	15440,68044,35028
3	04771,21254,71966	36	15563,02500,76729
4	06020,59991,32796	37	15682,01724,06700
5	06989,70004,33602	38	15797,83596,61681
6	07781,51250,38364	39	15910,64607,02650
7	08450,98040,01426	40	16020,59991,32796
8	09030,89986,99194	41	16127,83856,71974
9	09542,42509,43932	2	16232,49290,39790
10	10000,00000,00000	43	16334,68455,57959

Some of Henry Briggs's logarithms

Pierre de Fermat

Pierre de Fermat (1601–65) spent most of his life in Toulouse as a lawyer. He considered mathematics as a hobby, published little, and communicated with other scientists by letter. Fermat was the first important European number theorist since Greek times and resurrected the subject with some stunning results. His other main area of interest was analytic geometry, which he helped to introduce.

Fermat was born in Beaumont-de-Lomagne in the south of France and attended the University of Toulouse. After receiving a Bachelor of Civil Law degree from Orléans in 1631, he spent the rest of his life following a full-time career as a lawyer in Toulouse.

ANALYTIC GEOMETRY

Analytic geometry, in which we use algebraic techniques to help us solve geometrical problems, was born in 1637 and had two fathers: René Descartes and Pierre de Fermat. Fermat, in particular, gave a successful new method of finding tangents to curves; this used ideas and techniques of approximation taken from Diophantus's *Arithmetica*, which had recently been published in French (see opposite).

Pierre de Fermat

NUMBER THEORY

Although Fermat made substantial contributions to the development of analytic geometry, he is mainly remembered for his contributions to number theory, even though he often stated his results without proof and did not publish his conclusions.

FERMAT PRIMES

Fermat conjectured that if n is a power of 2, then $2^n + 1$ is a prime number. The first few of these numbers are indeed prime: $2^1 + 1 = 3$, $2^2 + 1 = 5$, $2^4 + 1 = 17$, $2^8 + 1 = 257$, $2^{16} + 1 = 65,537$. But Euler proved that $2^{32} + 1$ is divisible by 641, and no other Fermat primes have ever been found.

THE $4n + 1$ THEOREM

Let us list all prime numbers of the form $4n + 1$ (that is, each is one more than a multiple of 4):

5, 13, 17, 29, 37, 41, 53, 61, …

Fermat observed that:

Every prime number in this list can be written as the sum of two perfect squares:
for example, $13 = 4 + 9 = 2^2 + 3^2$
and $41 = 16 + 25 = 4^2 + 5^2$

Fermat stated this result without proof. It was left for later mathematicians to prove it.

PELL'S EQUATION

Earlier we saw that Brahmagupta found integer solutions to "Pell's equation" $Cx^2 + 1 = y^2$, for several specific values of C. His work was continued by Fermat, who managed to find a solution in the difficult case $C = 109$ and challenged his mathematical contemporaries to do the same. Since the smallest solution is:

$$x = 15{,}140{,}424{,}455{,}100$$
$$y = 158{,}070{,}671{,}986{,}249$$

it is clear that Fermat must have had a general method for finding such solutions, but he never revealed it to anyone.

FERMAT'S "LITTLE THEOREM"

Another result of Fermat concerns certain large numbers that are divisible by primes. To illustrate it, we choose a prime number, such as 37, and then choose any positive integer, such as 14. Fermat's result tells us that if we were to calculate the number $14^{37} - 14$, then the result can be divided exactly by 37. In general, Fermat's "little theorem" tells us that:

Given any prime number p and any whole number n, the number $n^p - n$ can be divided exactly by p.

This is not simply a theoretical fact—it now forms the basis of important recent work in cryptography and internet security.

FERMAT'S "LAST THEOREM"

We have seen that there are integers x, y, and z satisfying the equation $x^2 + y^2 = z^2$ (the *Pythagorean triples*): for example, we could take $x = 3$, $y = 4$ and $z = 5$, since $3^2 + 4^2 = 5^2$.

But is it possible to find integers x, y, and z that satisfy the equations $x^3 + y^3 = z^3$ and $x^4 + y^4 = z^4$, or (in general) $x^n + y^n = z^n$, for any larger number n?

In his copy of Diophantus's *Arithmetica*, Fermat claimed to have "an admirable proof which this margin is too narrow to contain" of the statement that:

For any integer n (greater than 2), there do not exist positive integers x, y, and z for which $x^n + y^n = z^n$.

Using a method known as the "method of infinite descent" which he devised, Fermat proved this for $n = 4$, but it seems rather unlikely that he had a general argument that works for all values of n.

As we shall see later in the book, *Fermat's last theorem* (as it became known) was finally proved in September 1994 by Andrew Wiles and published in 1995. It had been a long and difficult struggle.

An Illustration of Fermat's Approach

Fermat used approximations to find the maximum and minimum values of certain expressions. One of his problems was to find the point E on a line AC, for which the product $AE \times EC$ takes its maximum value.

Let $AC = b$ and $AE = a$; then $EC = b - a$ and the product $AE \times EC = a \times (b - a)$.

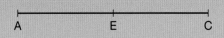

Fermat's idea was that when the position of E gives the maximum value, then this product does not change much if E is moved slightly, say by an amount e.

So $a \times (b - a)$ is approximately equal to $(a + e) \times (b - a - e)$.

When this is the case, be is approximately equal to $2ae + e^2$ and, on dividing through by e, we see that b is approximately equal to $2a + e$.

Then Fermat wrote:

Suppressing e: b = 2a. To solve the problem we must take the half of b.

So the maximum value of the product occurs when E is the midpoint of the line AC.

René Descartes

René Descartes (1596–1650) was born in Touraine in France, trained as a lawyer in Poitiers, and died in Stockholm while tutor to Queen Christina of Sweden. In common with many other seventeenth-century thinkers, he sought a symbolism to discover truths about the world, and he saw algebraic language as a way forward that might have wider application. Cartesian coordinates are named after him.

René Descartes' ground-breaking mathematics appears in his *Discours de la Méthode* (Discourse on Method) (1637), a philosophical treatise on universal science. It had three appendices: one on optics (containing the first published statement of the law of refraction), one on metereology (containing an explanation of primary and secondary rainbows), and one on geometry, extending to a hundred pages and containing fundamental contributions to analytic geometry.

La Géométrie generated great excitement and had considerable influence through its use of algebraic methods to solve geometrical problems. This set in train a gradual movement from geometry toward algebra that continued for about one hundred years, culminating in the work of Leonhard Euler.

LA GÉOMÉTRIE

Descartes first introduced a simplification by considering all quantities as non-dimensional, whereas geometers had previously dealt with lengths and considered the product of two lengths as an area.

He then claimed to be able to solve geometrical problems by algebra and he believed that solutions to algebraic equations could also be obtained by geometrical construction. As an example of such a construction he showed how to use lines and a circle to obtain a solution to a quadratic equation, as follows.

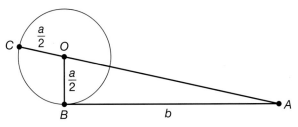

The length of AC is the positive solution of the quadratic equation $x^2 = ax + b^2$

He then illustrated his algebraic approach by solving an ancient geometrical problem of Pappus, who had asked for the path traced by a point moving in a specified way relative to a number of fixed lines. Descartes named two particular lengths x and y and then calculated all the other lengths in terms of them, thereby obtaining a equation involving the terms x^2, xy,

René Descartes

and y^2; this is a quadratic equation, and shows that the required path is a conic, as below.

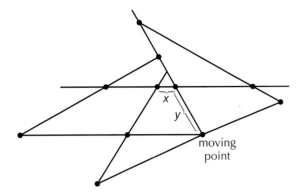

Solving Pappus's problem

Descartes also developed a method for finding tangents to curves which reduced the problem to finding solutions of a certain type of algebraic equation. However, at no stage did he introduce the "Cartesian coordinates" (with axes at right angles) that are usually named after him, with the points represented by pairs of numbers (x, y) and the lines represented by linear equations of the form $y = mx + c$.

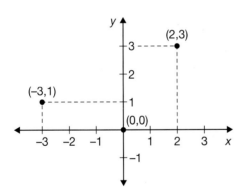

Cartesian coordinates

TWO MATHEMATICAL CONTRIBUTIONS

Descartes invented a "rule of signs" for locating the roots of polynomial equations. Note that, as we move from left to right, the equation

$$x^4 - x^3 - 19x^2 + 49x - 30 = 0$$

has three changes of sign (between − and +, or + and −) and one pair of like signs (both −). Descartes' rule asserts that, in this situation, the

equation has at most three positive solutions and at most one negative solution.

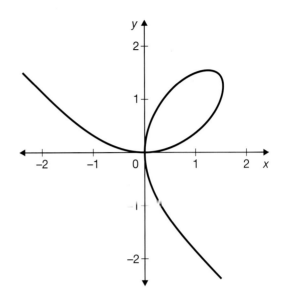

He also analyzed various geometrical curves. One of these was the above *folium of Descartes,* with equation $x^3 + y^3 = 3xy$.

DESCARTES' VORTEX THEORY

Descartes also developed an influential theory of planetary motion in which vortices (whirlpools) fill space and push the planets around in their orbits (see below). This theory was later dismissed by Isaac Newton in his *Principia Mathematica.*

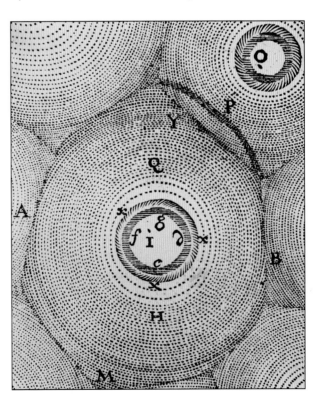

Blaise Pascal

Blaise Pascal (1623–62) contributed to several areas of mathematics, as well as to science and religious philosophy. He laid the foundations for the theory of probability, wrote about atmospheric pressure, discovered his "hexagon theorem" in projective geometry, and built a calculating machine. He also wrote an influential treatise on the array of numbers now known as "Pascal's triangle."

Blaise Pascal was born in Clermont-Ferrand in the Auverne region of France, and showed his mathematical ability from an early age. His father Étienne, a tax official, lawyer, and amateur mathematician, assumed responsibility for his son's education and took him to Paris to attend the scientific meetings arranged by Marin Mersenne.

PASCAL'S CALCULATING MACHINE

In 1642 Pascal built a calculating machine (known as "The Pascaline") to help in his father's work. Although it could only add or subtract, using "carry-over" gearing, it was well documented—indeed, many later machines were only slight modifications of it.

PROBABILITY THEORY

The modern theory of probability is often considered to begin in 1654, arising out of some correspondence between Pascal and Fermat over gambling problems. One particular problem was

raised by the Chevalier of Méré and concerns the fair division of the stakes in a game when it is interrupted before its conclusion.

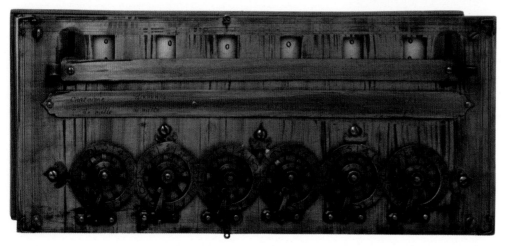

Above: *Blasie Pascal*
Left: *The Pascaline could deal with numbers up to 9,999,999, but could only be used for addition and subtraction. It was operated by moving the dials, the solution to the problem appearing in the windows above.*

Suppose that two players agree to play a certain game repeatedly; the winner, who wins $100, is the one who first wins six times. If the game is interrupted when one player has won five games and the other player has won four games, how should the $100 be divided fairly between the players? (The answer is that the one with five wins receives $75 and the other receives $25.) Pascal gave the general solution in more detail in his *Traité du Triangle Arithmétique* (Treatise on the Arithmetical Triangle) of 1654.

THE ARITHMETICAL TRIANGLE

The arithmetical triangle, now called *Pascal's triangle*, was known to Islamic, Indian, and Chinese mathematicians many centuries earlier. But to credit Pascal is justifiable because he carried out the first systematic investigation into its properties.

Over the centuries the numbers in this array arose in various different ways.

PATTERNS OF NUMBERS

The arithmetical triangle has several interesting numerical features. For example, the first diagonal ($k = 0$) is a sequence of 1s, and the next two diagonals ($k = 1$ and 2) contain the natural numbers 1, 2, 3, … and the triangular numbers 1, 3, 6, 10, … .

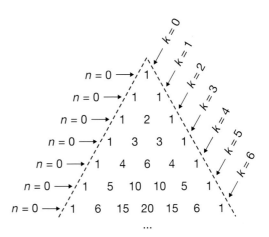

The first few rows of Pascal's triangle

Moreover, each number (apart from the outside 1s) is the sum of the two numbers above it; for example, the number 20 in the seventh row ($n = 6$) is the sum of the two 10s above it.

Another interesting feature is that the sum of the entries in each row is a power of 2; for example, in the sixth row ($n = 5$):

$$1 + 5 + 10 + 10 + 5 + 1 = 32 = 2^5$$

Pascal proved this result using a method, now called *mathematical induction*, which he was the first to express explicitly.

BINOMIAL COEFFICIENTS

The numbers appearing in the triangle are all binomial coefficients. These numbers arise in the expansions of the various powers of $1 + x$:

$$(1 + x)^0 = 1$$
$$(1 + x)^1 = 1 + 1x$$
$$(1 + x)^2 = 1 + 2x + 1x^2$$
$$(1 + x)^3 = 1 + 3x + 3x^2 + 1x^3$$
$$(1 + x)^4 = 1 + 4x + 6x^2 + 4x^3 + 1x^4$$
$$(1 + x)^5 = 1 + 5x + 10x^2 + 10x^3 + 5x^4 + 1x^5$$
$$(1 + x)^6 = 1 + 6x + 15x^2 + 20x^3 + 15x^4 + 6x^5 + 1x^6$$

COMBINATIONS

The numbers in the triangle also arise as the number of different ways of making selections; for example, the number of different four-member teams that can be chosen from six people is written $C(6, 4)$ and is 15. In general, $C(n, k)$ is the number in row n and diagonal k, and is equal to $n! / k! (n - k)!$.

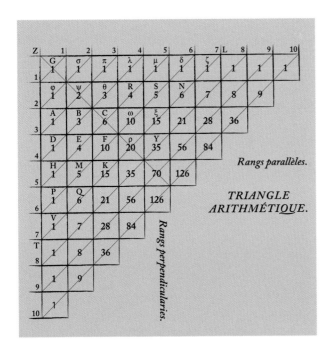

Pascal's drawing of his triangle (adapted from his posthumous publication of 1665)

Cavalieri and Roberval

During the seventeenth century, much progress was made on the two branches of the infinitesimal calculus, the seemingly unrelated areas now called differentiation *and* integration. *Bonaventura Cavalieri (1598–1647) developed a theory of "indivisibles" that provided a systematic way to help in the calculation of certain areas. Gilles Personne de Roberval (1602–75) was a French scientist who also discovered powerful techniques for calculating areas.*

Cavalieri, an Italian mathematician, was held in high regard by Galileo, who declared:

Few, if any, since Archimedes, have delved as far and as deep into the science of geometry.

In 1629, Galileo helped Cavalieri to obtain a professorship at Bologna, which was renewed every three years until his death.

Roberval at the Paris Academy of Sciences, 1666

CAVALIERI'S PRINCIPLE

Cavalieri wrote ten books on mathematics and science and published a table of logarithms. His most important work was his *Geometria Indivisibilibus Continuorum Nova Quadam Ratione Promota* (A Certain Method for the Development of a New Geometry of Continuous Indivisibles), which appeared in 1635.

Cavalieri considered a geometrical object to be made up of objects of one dimension lower, the indivisibles, so an area was made up from lines and a solid object was made up from planes. The problem was then how to compare the indivisibles of one geometrical object with those of another.

Cavalieri's principle set out circumstances in which this can be done. In the case of areas it says that:

Two plane figures have the same area if they lie between the same parallel lines, and any line drawn parallel to the given two lines cuts off equal chords in each figure.

Cavalieri used this principle to find the area under the curve $y = x^n$, where n is a given positive integer.

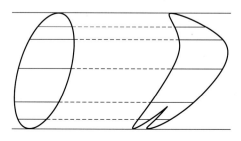

Cavalieri's principle for plane figures

The Route to the Calculus

Many other seventeenth-century mathematicians, such as Kepler, Fermat, Descartes, and Pascal, found tangents to curves and areas under curves. There were also contributions from:

- Gregory of St Vincent, a Belgian mathematician who found the area under the hyperbola $y = x^{-1}$.

- John Wallis, who found the area under the curve $y = x^k$, when k is a positive fraction.

- Evangelista Torricelli, a student of Galileo and the inventor of the barometer, who found areas and tangents and studied the parabolic paths of projectiles. In going from an equation for "distance in terms of time" to one of "speed in terms of time," and conversely, he became aware of the inverse nature of tangent and area problems.

- Isaac Barrow (Newton's predecessor as Lucasian Professor of Mathematics in Cambridge), who also studied the inverse relationship between these problems.

However, it was Newton and Leibniz who transcended what anyone had done before, and independently created what today we call the calculus:

- *differentiation*—a systematic way of obtaining slopes of tangents to curves;

- *integration*—a systematic way of obtaining areas under curves;

- the *inverse relationship between these tangent and area problems*—namely, that differentiation and integration are inverse processes: if you integrate an expression and then differentiate the result, you get back to where you started, and *vice versa*.

ROBERVAL AND THE CYCLOID

Cavalieri's principle was widely viewed as both useful and powerful. Roberval made impressive use of the principle (claiming to have discovered it independently) to calculate the area under one arch of a *cycloid*—the curve traced by a fixed point on a circle rolling along a straight line; one can imagine a cycloid by picturing the curve traced out by a piece of mud on a bicycle tyre when the bicycle is wheeled along.

Roberval proved that the area under one arch of a cycloid is exactly three times that of the area of the generating circle. To do this, he showed

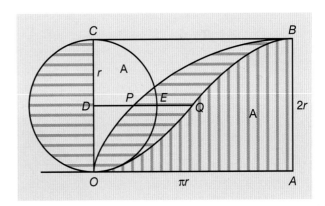

Roberval's cycloid

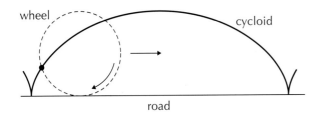

A cycloid

that the two horizontally shaded regions below have the same area, and noted that the vertically shaded area is one-half that of the rectangle OABC. He deduced that the area under one-half of the cycloid is:

$$\tfrac{1}{2}\pi r^2 + \tfrac{1}{2}(2r \times \pi r) = \tfrac{3}{2}\pi r^2$$

It follows that the total area under one arch of the cycloid is $3\pi r^2$, which is three times the area of the circle.

Christiaan Huygens

The 1650s saw a shift in the center of mathematical activity away from France. The Netherlands and Britain were now the leading countries, and foremost among Dutch mathematicians was Christiaan Huygens (1629–95). With his construction of the first pendulum clock, Huygens considerably improved the accuracy of time-measurement. He also contributed to geometry, mechanics, astronomy, and probability.

Huygens belonged to a prominent and well-connected Dutch family. He studied law and mathematics, first at the University of Leiden and then at the College of Orange at Breda. His first works in the 1650s were on mathematics, studying the cissoid and conchoids (classical curves studied by the Greeks).

PENDULUM CLOCKS

The need for clocks to measure time accurately was important in astronomy and navigation. A recurring interest of Huygens was the development of such clocks, and his most famous discovery was in this area.

For a pendulum bob, the period of oscillation is only approximately independent of the amplitude (or extent) of the oscillation, although this inaccuracy is often ignored when the amplitude is small. Huygens discovered that:

> *For a cycloid whose axis is erected on the perpendicular and whose vertex is located at the bottom, the times of descent, in which a body arrives at the lowest point at the vertex after having departed from any point on the cycloid, are equal to each other…*

This means that, if the path of a pendulum could be made to follow a cycloidal path, its period of oscillation would be independent of its amplitude.

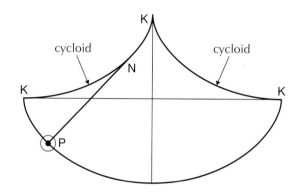

A pendulum bob following a cycloidal path

Huygens achieved this by having two "cheeks" from the point of suspension of the pendulum along which the cord wraps itself as the pendulum swings. The shapes of these cheeks are also cycloids; their precise form depends on the length of the pendulum.

PROBABILITY

In 1655 Huygens became interested in probability during a visit to Paris and, encouraged by Pascal, wrote *De Ratiociniis in Ludo Aleae* (On the Values in Games of Chance), published in 1657. This was the first systematic treatment of probability theory, and remained the only one available until the eighteenth century. As Huygens remarked:

> *Although in a pure game of chance the results are uncertain, the chance that one player has to win or lose depends on a determined value.*

Christiaan Huygens

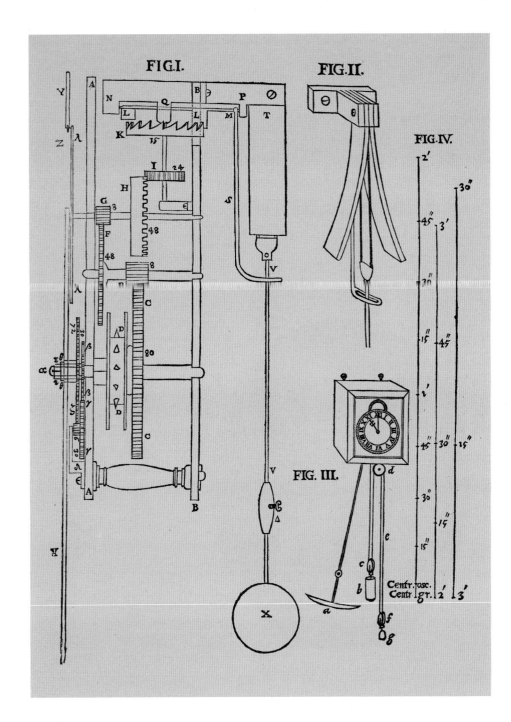

Left: *Huygens' drawings of clock mechanisms, from his* Horologium Oscillatorium *(The Pendulum Clock) of 1673*

The answer lies between 24 and 25: after 24 throws the probability of throwing a double-six is slightly less than ½; after 25 throws it is slightly greater than ½.

ASTRONOMY AND MOTION

In cooperation with his brother, Huygens developed great expertise in the grinding and polishing of lenses. This led to them making the best telescopes of the time, which enabled Huygens to discover, in 1655, the moon of Saturn now called Titan. In the following year he presented his description of the rings of Saturn:

His "determined value" is what we now call the *expectation*, the average expected winnings if the game were played many times.

An illustration of his first principle is that if in a game one has an equal chance of winning $x or $y, then the expected winnings would be $½(x + y). This is the stake that a player should be prepared to bet to play the game.

Huygens also discussed a problem raised in correspondence between Pascal and Fermat:

How many times should a pair of dice be thrown so as to give at least an even chance of obtaining a double-six?

It is surrounded by a thin flat ring, nowhere touching and inclined to the ecliptic.

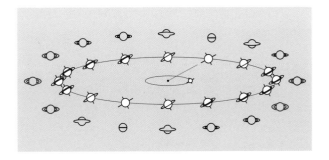

A diagram from Huygens' Systema Saturnium *(1659), showing the orbit of Saturn*

Isaac Newton

Sir Isaac Newton (1642–1727) remains unchallenged in the depth and breadth of his mathematical and scientific work. He obtained the general form of the binomial theorem, explained the relationship between differentiation and integration, studied power series, and analyzed cubic curves. In gravitation, Newton asserted that the force that causes objects on earth to fall is the same as the one that keeps the planets orbiting around the sun, and that they are governed by a universal inverse-square law of force.

Isaac Newton was born on Christmas Day 1642 in Woolsthorpe, a hamlet in Lincolnshire, England. He went to Cambridge University where he was later appointed Lucasian Professor at the age of twenty-six, staying in post until 1696 when he moved to London to become Warden, and then Master, of the Royal Mint. He became President of the Royal Society in 1703.

NEWTON'S MATHEMATICAL WORKS

CALCULUS

Newton's creation of the calculus was involved with movement—how things change with time, or "flow." His tangent problems involved velocities, and in his *Treatise on Fluxions* (circulated to his friends, but not published until after his death) he gave rules for calculating these velocities. For area problems he did not use a direct approach, but instead regarded them as inverse problems.

INFINITE SERIES

An infinite series is similar to a polynomial, except that it goes on for ever—for example:

$$1 - 2x + 3x^2 - 4x^3 + 5x^4 - 6x^5 + \ldots$$

Newton's realization of the importance and use of infinite series was a major contribution to mathematics. Particularly useful was his general binomial theorem which gives the expansion of $(1 + x)^n$ as an infinite series when n is not a positive integer—for example, the infinite series illustrated above is the binomial expansion of $(1 + x)^{-2}$.

CUBIC CURVES

The classification of quadratic curves was well known—they are the conic sections—but the classification of cubic curves was much more difficult. Newton achieved it by showing that all seventy-eight different types of them can be obtained by projection from one of a family of five.

Above: *Isaac Newton*
Below: *Two of Newton's cubic curves*

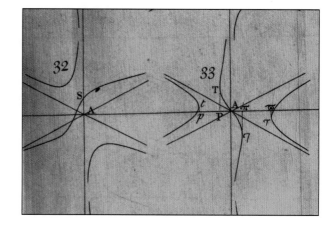

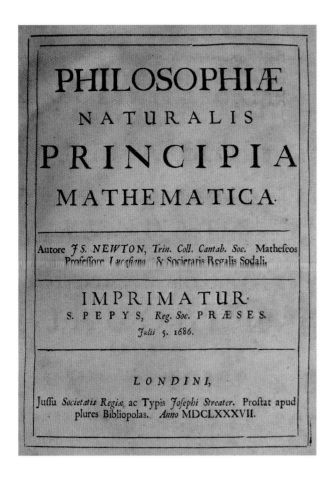

- Every body continues in its state of rest, or of uniform motion in a right line, unless it is compelled to change that state by forces impressed on it.

- Any change of motion is proportional to the force, and is made in the direction of the line in which the force is applied.

- To any action there is an equal and opposite reaction.

account for the orbits of comets, the variation of tides, and the flattening of the earth at its poles due to the earth's rotation.

In his *Principia* Newton also considered the movement of objects in resisting media and the velocity needed to project an object so as to put it into orbit around the earth.

Newton achieved honor and reverence in his own lifetime. Alexander Pope's well-known epitaph expresses the reverence with which Newton's contemporaries viewed him:

Nature, and Nature's Laws lay hid in Night.
God said, Let Newton be! And All was light.

PRINCIPIA MATHEMATICA

The celebrated story of the apple, which Newton recounted in old age, is part of scientific folklore. Seeing an apple fall, he apparently suggested that the gravitational force that pulls the apple to earth is the same as the force that keeps the moon orbiting around the earth and the earth orbiting around the sun. Moreover, this planetary motion is governed by a universal law of gravitation, the inverse-square law:

The force of attraction between two objects varies as the product of their masses, and inversely as the square of the distance between them.

So if each mass is trebled then the force increases by a factor of 9, and if the distance between them is multiplied by 10 then the force decreases by a factor of 100.

In his *Philosophiae Naturalis Principia Mathematica* (Mathematical Principles of Natural Philosophy) (1687), possibly the greatest scientific work of all time, Newton used this law and his three laws of motion to explain Kepler's three laws of elliptical planetary motion and to

Newton's memorial in Westminster Abbey, London

Gottfried Leibniz

Gottfried Wilhelm Leibniz (1646–1716) was the greatest theorist of logic and language since Aristotle, and a mathematician and philosopher of the highest rank. He was guided in his investigations by the desire for a "logic of discovery" and a language that would reflect the structure of the world. This showed itself in his work on binary arithmetic, symbolic logic, his calculus, and his calculating machine.

Leibniz was born in Leipzig in Germany and went to the University there at the early age of fourteen (where his father was professor of moral philosophy), and after that to Altdorf, where he took his doctoral degree while still only twenty. He was exceptionally talented, with wide-ranging interests across many disciplines, but did not obtain an academic position after leaving university. He spent forty years in rather minor positions, traveling around Europe and representing the interests of the Elector of Mainz and the Duke of Hanover.

BINARY ARITHMETIC

Following ideas of Ramón Lull, Leibniz set out his guiding inspiration in an essay of 1666, the intention to devise:

A general method in which all truths of the reason would be reduced to a kind of calculation.

His binary arithmetic was an example of the attempt to reduce complex ideas to their simplest forms, and around 1679 he wrote that, instead of the decimal system:

It is possible to use in its place a binary system, so that as soon as we have reached two we start again from unity in this way:

(0)	(1)	(2)	(3)	(4)	(5)	(6)	(7)	(8)
0	1	10	11	100	101	110	111	1000

… what a wonderful way all numbers are expressed by unity and nothing.

Such binary representations are now routinely used by modern computers.

CALCULATING MACHINE

Leibniz's calculating machine shows another aspect of his plan, in which he wished to use mechanical calculation to find a way to error-free truth. The machine's crucial innovation was a stepped gearing wheel with a variable number of teeth along its length, which allowed multiplication on turning a handle. Leibniz's stepped wheel was an important component of mechanical calculators until they were replaced by electronic calculators.

THE CALCULUS

Leibniz's calculus was by far his most ambitious and influential work, and again arose from his

Gottfried Leibniz

The Priority Dispute

Who invented the calculus first?

Newton was probably the first to discover his results on the calculus, but although he circulated his discoveries privately to his friends, they were not published until after his death.

Leibniz, working independently, introduced his superior notation in 1675 and published his results on the differential calculus in 1684 and on the integral calculus in 1686. In the latter paper, he also explained the inverse relationship between differentiation and integration.

This led to a bitter priority dispute between Newton and Leibniz, with Newton's followers accusing Leibniz of plagiarism. With much ill-feeling between Britain and the Continent on this issue, Newton (as President of the Royal Society) arranged for an "independent" commission to investigate the issue. It was not Newton's finest hour: he personally chose the members of the commission, writing much of the evidence for them to consider, and the commission unsurprisingly ruled in his favor.

desire to find general symbolic methods for uncovering truths.

Leibniz's calculus originated in a different manner from that of Newton's, being based on sums and differences, rather than on velocity and motion.

In 1675 Leibniz introduced two symbols that would for ever be used in calculus. One was his d (or dy/dx) notation for differentiation, referring to a decrease in dimension—for example, from areas (x^2) to lengths (x). The other was the integral sign: attempting to find areas under curves by summing lines, he defined *omnia l* (all the *l*s), which he then represented by an elongated *S* for sum: this is the symbol $\int$ for the integral sign.

It will be useful to write $\int$ for omn...

Leibniz presented algebraic rules for differentiation which can then be used to find tangents, and to locate maxima and minima. As well as giving the rules, he also differentiated powers of x:

$d(x^a) = a\, x^{a-1} dx$, where a is any fraction
– so $d(x^2) = 2x\, dx$ and $d(x^{1/2}) = \tfrac{1}{2}\, x^{-1/2}\, dx$

LEIBNIZ'S RULES FOR DIFFERENTIATION

- For any constant a:
  $d(a) = 0,\ d(ax) = a\, dx$
- $d(v + y) = dv + dy$
- $d(vy) = v\, dy + y\, dv$
- $d(v/y) = (y\, dv - v\, dy)\, /\, y^2$

These rules are easy to use—for example, we can use them to differentiate:

$w = x^{1/2}/(x^2 + 4)$

In the last rule, let $v = x^{1/2}$ and $y = x^2 + 4$. Then:

$dw = \{(x^2 + 4)\, d(x^{1/2}) - x^{1/2}\, d(x^2 + 4)\}\, /\, (x^2 + 4)^2.$

By the second rule:

$d(x^2 + 4) = d(x^2) + d(4) = d(x^2) + d(4) = d(x^2),$
since $d(4) = 0$, by the first rule.

Finally, on substituting:

$d(x^2) = 2x\, dx$ and $d(x^{1/2}) = \tfrac{1}{2}\, x^{-1/2}\, dx$

we get:

$dw = ((x^2 + 4).\tfrac{1}{2}x^{-1/2}\, dx - x^{1/2}.2x\, dx)\, /\, (x^2 + 4)^2.$

which can be rearranged as:

$dw = \{(2 - \tfrac{3}{2}x^2)\, /\, x^{1/2}.(x^2 + 4)^2\}\, dx.$

Left: *Leibniz's calculating machine*

Jacob Bernoulli

In the entire history of science and mathematics it is hard to find a more prominent family than the Bernoullis. Its first distinguished member was Jacob Bernoulli (1654–1705), who was born in Basel in Switzerland and later became professor of mathematics there in 1687. He had a wide range of interests, investigating infinite series, the cycloid, transcendental curves, the logarithmic spiral, and the catenary, and introduced the term integral. *His posthumous text on probability contains the celebrated law of large numbers.*

Jacob Bernoulli remained as Professor of Mathematics at Basel until his death, when he was succeeded by his brother Johann. The Bernoulli brothers were the foremost advocates of the Leibnizian calculus, publicizing it, publishing on it, and applying it to solve new problems.

Jacob confirmed that the harmonic series:

$$1 + \tfrac{1}{2} + \tfrac{1}{3} + \tfrac{1}{4} + \tfrac{1}{5} + \tfrac{1}{6} + \ldots$$

does not converge to a finite number, while the series:

$$1 + (\tfrac{1}{2})^2 + (\tfrac{1}{3})^2 + (\tfrac{1}{4})^2 + (\tfrac{1}{5})^2 + (\tfrac{1}{6})^2 + \ldots$$

converges—but he could not find its sum.

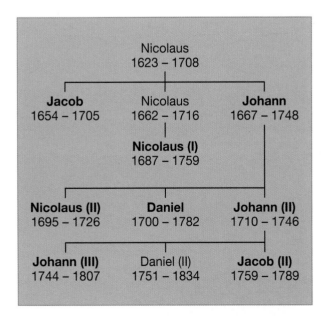

The Bernoulli mathematical dynasty, with eight mathematicians in bold type

Jacob Bernoulli

The brothers Jacob and Johann competed fiercely and publicly. On one occasion, Jacob posed the problem of finding the shape that a heavy chain takes up when hung between two points. Galileo had incorrectly thought it to be a parabola, and Johann was delighted to beat his brother to the correct answer, which is a curve that we call a *catenary*.

A catenary

ARS CONJECTANDI

Jacob Bernoulli's book on probability, *Ars Conjectandi* (Art of Conjecturing), was his most important and influential publication. It was the culmination of twenty years' work and was published in 1713, eight years after his death.

The first three parts of the book build on previous work—indeed, the first part is a commentary on Huygens' earlier treatment. Here, he calculated the sums of integer powers (squares, cubes …), obtaining a general result involving what are now called the *Bernoulli numbers*.

JACOBI BERNOULLI,
Profeff. Bafil. & utriufque Societ. Reg. Scientiae
Gall. & Pruff. Sodal.
MATHEMATICI CELEBERRIMI,

ARS CONJECTANDI,

OPUS POSTHUMUM.

Accedit

TRACTATUS
DE SERIEBUS INFINITIS,

Et Epistola Gallicé scripta

DE LUDO PILÆ
RETICULARIS.

BASILEÆ,
Impenfis THURNISIORUM, Fratrum.
cIↃ IↃcc xIII.

The last part was very innovative. His central concern was how to quantify probabilities in situations where it was impossible to list or count all possibilities. His approach was to see what happened in similar situations:

For example, if we have observed that out of 300 persons of the same age and with the same constitution as a certain Titius, 200 died within ten years while the rest survived, we can with reasonable certainty conclude that there are twice as many chances that Titius will have to pay his debt to nature within the ensuing decade as there are chances that he will live beyond that time.

Bernoulli believed that the more observations we make, the better we can predict future outcomes, and he quantified this in his *law of large numbers*. He showed that increases in the number of observations enable us to estimate the probability to any degree of accuracy, and he calculated how many observations are needed so that we are sure to be within a predefined degree of accuracy. To do this involved working with sums of binomial coefficients.

THE LOGARITHMIC SPIRAL

Bernoulli was interested in the logarithmic spiral and called it *spira mirabilis* (the marvelous spiral). It has the property that the tangent at each point makes a fixed angle with the line joining the point to the center. This spiral has pleasing symmetries, reproducing itself under various transformations—for example, each arm of the spiral has the same shape as the previous one, but is larger.

Bernoulli asked for this spiral to be carved on his tombstone, with the inscription *EADEM MUTATA RESURGO* (I arise the same, though changed). It appears at the bottom of the tombstone (*see right*).

Johann Bernoulli

Johann Bernoulli (1667–1748), the younger brother of Jacob, was a prolific mathematician who tutored the Marquis de l'Hôpital and Leonhard Euler. He posed many problems in connection with the priority debate between Newton and Leibniz, and of these, the most significant for the development of mathematics was that of the brachistochrone—*finding the curve of quickest descent. Bernoulli was called the "Archimedes of his age," and this is inscribed on his tombstone.*

Johann Bernoulli was born and died in Basel. He developed Leibniz's techniques in the 1690s and with Huygens' support occupied the chair of mathematics at Groningen (Holland) from 1695 until 1705, when he succeeded his brother in Basel.

Johann Bernoulli

THE CALCULUS

Before moving to Groningen, Bernoulli was employed in France as tutor to the Marquis de l'Hôpital in the Leibnizian calculus. This resulted in l'Hôpital's *Analyse des Infiniment Petits, pour l'Intelligence des Lignes Courbes* (The Analysis of the Infinitely Small, for the Understanding of Curved Lines) (1696), the first printed book on the differential calculus. It contained many of Johann's results, including a result for calculating limits now usually known as *l'Hôpital's rule*. The Marquis credited Bernoulli in his preface:

> *I must own myself very much obliged to the labors of Messieurs Bernoulli, but particularly to those of the present Professor at Groeningen, as having made free with their Discoveries as well as those of Mr Leibniz: so that whatever they please to claim as their own I frankly return them.*

Johann, however, considered that this had been done in a rather offhand manner.

Bernoulli's comprehensive work on the integral calculus was published in 1742, although most of it had been written by 1700. He defined integration as the inverse of differentiation and gave several techniques for evaluating integrals. He explained that its main use was in finding areas, and then used it to solve *inverse tangent problems*, in which we are given some property of the tangent to a curve at each point and are asked to find the curve. Most importantly, Bernoulli showed how to recast problems in geometry or mechanics in the language of the calculus; this caused inverse tangent problems to become known as *differential equations*, because they were recast as equations involving differentials.

THE BRACHISTOCHRONE PROBLEM

In June 1696 Bernoulli proposed the following "new problem which mathematicians are invited to solve," concerning an object descending under gravity along a curve from a point A to a point B:

> *If two points A and B are given in a vertical plane, to assign to a mobile particle M the path AMB along which, descending under its own weight, it passes from the point A to the point B in the briefest time.*

At first, one might think that the "curve of quickest descent" from *A* to *B* is the straight line joining them, but this is not the case—and nor do we achieve the shortest time if the curve is too steep to start with and too flat later on. The desired compromise between these is known as the *brachistochrone*, from the Greek words for "shortest time."

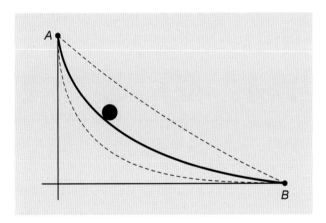

Using an optical analogy, Bernoulli deduced that at each point on the desired curve, the sine of the angle between the tangent to the curve and the vertical axis is proportional to the square root of the distance fallen. This gave rise to the differential equation:

$$dy/dx = \sqrt{x} / (1 - x)$$

which he then solved to show that the desired curve is a *cycloid*, the curve that Roberval had

studied and that Huygens used in constructing his pendulum clock.

The brachistochrone problem was answered by Jacob Bernoulli, Leibniz, and Newton. Jacob Bernoulli showed, by using the calculus, that no matter where an object starts on this curve, it descends to the bottom after the same amount of time. Newton solved the problem overnight and sent his solution anonymously, but on seeing it, Johann Bernoulli identified Newton's style, saying that "I recognize the lion by his claw."

The brachistochrone problem gave rise to new strands of mathematics. Jacob Bernoulli's method for solving it used an approach that initiated a whole new field, the calculus of variations, in which one seeks a curve that satisfies a given maximum or minimum property—here, the cycloid minimizes the time of descent.

Meanwhile, arising out of his investigations into the curve of quickest descent, Johann posed the problem of finding two families of curves with the property that each curve in the first family meets each curve in the second family at right angles. These are called *orthogonal families*, and led to new concepts in thinking about expressions that depend on more than one variable.

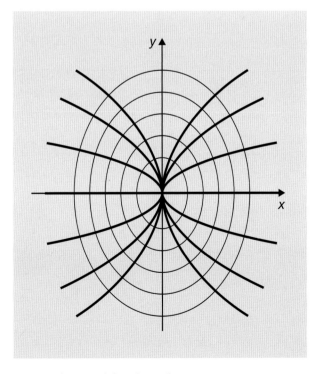

Two orthogonal families of curves

Jean le Rond d'Alembert

Jean le Rond d'Alembert (1717–83) was a leading Enlightenment figure. In his later years he wrote many of the mathematical and scientific articles for Denis Diderot's celebrated Encyclopédie, *which attempted to classify the knowledge of the time. Earlier, he had been the first to obtain the wave equation that describes the motion of a vibrating string. He also attempted to formalize the idea of a limit so as to put the calculus on a firm basis, and studied the convergence of infinite series, obtaining a result now known as the ratio test.*

As an infant, d'Alembert was abandoned by his mother outside the church of St Jean le Rond near Notre Dame in Paris—hence his name—and was brought up by the wife of a glazier. Although he qualified as a lawyer in 1738, his main interest was in mathematics. He was apparently a brilliant conversationalist and gifted with a superb memory. He was also quick to quarrel—with Clairault, Euler, and Daniel Bernoulli, among others.

THE *ENCYCLOPÉDIE*

The *Encyclopédie* was published between 1751 and 1777, with contributions from over 140 people, and consisted of over 70,000 articles. It was the major achievement of the French Enlightenment whose aim, in Diderot's words, was to "change the common way of thinking." D'Alembert was a leading member of the group of philosophers—*A Society of People of Letters*, as the title page shows—who produced this bible of the Enlightenment.

THE VIBRATING STRING

D'Alembert made notable contributions to the analysis of the motion of a vibrating string. If a string is stretched horizontally between two fixed

A vibrating string

points and made to vibrate, then, as he noted in a paper of 1747, the vertical displacement $u(x, t)$ of the string depends on both the horizontal distance x and the time t.

D'Alembert's contribution was to obtain a differential equation that describes the motion of the string. This was the first time that the techniques of the calculus had been deployed on a problem with more than one variable, and involves differentiation with respect to both x and t. The differential equation that he discovered is now called the wave equation:

$$c^2\, \partial^2 u(x, t)/\partial x^2 = \partial^2 u(x, t)/\partial t^2$$

where c is a constant that depends on the string.

D'Alembert solved this "partial differential equation" to find the motion of the string. His solutions were very general, but this is hardly surprising, since the string can be released from any initial shape with any initial velocity. His solution was:

$$u(x, t) = f(x + ct) + g(x - ct)$$

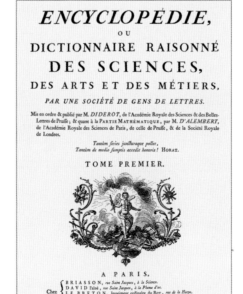

The first volume of the Encyclopédie

where *f* and *g* are arbitrary functions. As he remarked:

This equation contains an infinity of curves.

The question of how general such solution curves can be became one of the eighteenth century's most stimulating mathematical questions.

In 1752 d'Alembert tried to find solutions of the form:

a function of time × a function of distance

That is, $u(x, t) = F(t) \times G(x)$, where F depends on t and G depends on v. This converts the wave equation in two independent variables into two differential equations, each in one variable. These are easier to solve, and he deduced the solution:

$$u(x, t) = \cos(k\pi c/L)t \times \sin(v\pi/L)x$$

where L is the length of the string and k can be any positive integer. Different values of k

Jean le Rond d'Alembert

D'Alembert and the Idea of Limit

In his 1734 book *The Analyst*, Bishop Berkeley of Cloyne (in Ireland) had severely criticized the calculus of Newton and Leibniz for its shaky foundations. D'Alembert was concerned about such criticisms, and attempted to rescue the situation by basing the calculus on the idea of a "limit." In one of his contributions to the *Encyclopédie*, he wrote:

One says that one quantity is the limit of another quantity, when the second can approach the first more closely than any given quantity, however small, without the quantity approaching, passing the quantity which it approaches; so that the difference between a quantity and its limit is absolutely inassignable.

D'Alembert was only partially successful in his quest, and it was not until 1821 that the task was finally accomplished, by Augustin-Louis Cauchy.

give different modes of vibration with different frequencies.

It was Daniel Bernoulli, the son of Johann, who suggested that a vibrating string can exhibit infinitely many modes of vibration, all superimposed on each other. The solution is then the infinite sum:

$$u(x, t) = \alpha \cos(\pi c/L)t \sin(\pi/L)x$$
$$+ \beta \cos(2\pi c/L)t \sin(2\pi/L)x$$
$$+ \gamma \cos(3\pi c/L)t \sin(3\pi/L)x + \dots$$

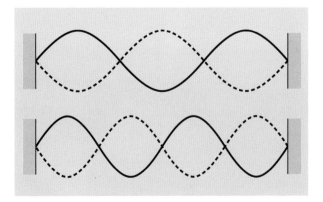

Two modes of vibration (k = 3 and 4)

Jean le Rond d'Alembert

Leonhard Euler

Leonhard Euler (1707–83) was the most prolific mathematician of all time. He produced over eight hundred books and papers in a wide range of areas, from such "pure" topics as number theory and the geometry of a circle, via mechanics, logarithms, infinite series, and calculus, to such practical concerns as optics, astronomy, and the stability of ships. He also introduced the symbols e for the exponential number, f for a function and i for √–1. In the words of Laplace: Read Euler, read Euler, he is the master of us all.

Euler's life can be conveniently divided into four periods. He spent his early years in Basel, Switzerland, entering the University there at the age of fourteen and receiving personal instruction from Johann Bernoulli. At the age of twenty he moved to Peter the Great's newly founded St Petersburg Academy, where he became head of the mathematics division. From 1741 to 1766 he was at Frederick the Great's Academy of Sciences in Berlin, before returning to St Petersburg for his final years.

EULER, THE POLYMATH

We now survey just a few of the myriad contributions that Euler made to mathematics.

Leonhard Euler

EULER'S BOOKS

Leonhard Euler wrote several ground-breaking books. His *Introductio in Analysin Infinitorum* (Introduction to the Analysis of Infinite Quantities) of 1748 expounded on infinite series, the exponential function, the properties of conics, partitions of numbers, and much else besides.

In 1755, he published a massive tome on the differential calculus, reformulating the subject in terms of the idea of a function and containing all the latest results, many due to him. He followed this, in 1768, with an influential three-volume work on the integral calculus, and in 1772 with a 775-page account of the motion of the moon.

His best-known work, still in print today, was his *Letters to a German Princess*, written from Berlin to the Princess of Anhalt-Dessau on a range of scientific topics.

INFINITE SERIES

While at St Petersburg, Euler became interested in infinite series. We have seen that the "harmonic series" of reciprocals has no finite sum, but Euler noticed that adding the first n terms of this series (up to $1/n$) gives a value very close to $\log_e n$. In fact, as he demonstrated, the difference between them:

$$(1 + \tfrac{1}{2} + \tfrac{1}{3} + \tfrac{1}{4} + \tfrac{1}{5} + \ldots + 1/n) - \log_e n$$

tends to a limiting value close to 0.577, now called *Euler's constant*.

A difficult mathematical problem of the time, which was known as the *Basel problem*, was to

The Exponential Function

We have all heard of "exponential growth," meaning something that grows very fast. Such growth arises in connection with compound interest or population growth, while there is "exponential decay" in the decay of radium or the cooling of a cup of tea.

Expressions such as 2^n or 3^n grow much faster than n^2 or n^3 as n increases; for example, if $n = 50$, then a computer calculating a million numbers per second can count up to $n^3 = 125{,}000$ in $\frac{1}{8}$ of a second, but would take 23 billion years to count up to 3^n.

In fact, mathematicians usually consider, not 2^n or 3^n, but e^n, where $e = 2.6182818\ldots$. The reason for choosing this strange number e is that if we plot the curve $y = e^x$, then *the slope of this curve at any point x is also e^x* – that is, $dy/dx = y$ for each point of the curve. Such a simple differential equation holds for $y = e^x$ and its multiples, but for no other curves.

The exponential function e^x turns up throughout mathematics and its applications – for example, Euler wrote it as a limit: e^x is the limit of $(1 + x/n)^n$, as x becomes large, and expanded as an infinite series:

$$e^x = 1 + x/1! + x^2/2! + x^3/3! + \ldots$$
in particular, $e = 1 + \frac{1}{1!} + \frac{1}{2!} + \frac{1}{3!} + \ldots$

Also, the exponential function is the inverse of the logarithm function: *if $y = e^x$, then $x = \log_e y$.*

Euler's most celebrated achievement was to extend the above infinite series to complex numbers, obtaining the result $e^{ix} = \cos x + i \sin x$, which intriguingly links the exponential function with the trigonometrical ones. A special case of this, relating the most important constants in mathematics, is $e^{i\pi} = -1$ or $e^{i\pi} + 1 = 0$.

find the sum of the reciprocals of the perfect squares:

$$1 + \frac{1}{4} + \frac{1}{9} + \frac{1}{16} + \frac{1}{25} + \ldots$$

The answer was known to be about 1.645, but no one could find its exact value. Euler achieved fame by showing that the sum is $\pi^2/6$. He then extended his calculations, ingeniously finding the sum of the reciprocals of all the 4th powers ($\pi^4/90$), the 6th powers ($\pi^6/945$), and so on, right up to the 26th powers!

MECHANICS

Throughout his life, Euler was interested in mechanics. In 1736, he published *Mechanica*, a 500-page treatise on the dynamics of a particle. Later, in work on the motion of rigid bodies, he obtained what we now call *Euler's equations of motion* and coined the phrase *moment of inertia*. Further results on mechanics were obtained in the 1770s. Much of this work used differential equations, an area to which Euler contributed a great deal.

THE BRIDGES OF KÖNIGSBERG

In 1735 Euler solved a well-known recreational problem. The city of Königsberg in East Prussia consisted of four regions joined by seven bridges, and its citizens used to entertain themselves by trying to cross each bridge exactly once. Can this be done?

Using a counting argument, involving the number of bridges emerging from each region, Euler proved that such a walk is impossible. He then extended his arguments to any arrangement of land areas and bridges.

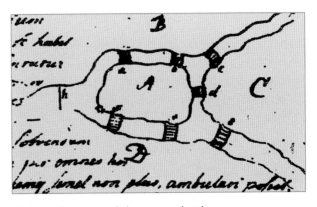

Euler's drawing of the seven bridges

Joseph-Louis Lagrange

Joseph-Louis Lagrange (1736–1813) excelled in all fields of analysis, number theory, and analytical and celestial mechanics. He wrote the first "theory of functions," using the idea of a power series to make the calculus more rigorous, and his writings on mechanics were also highly influential. In number theory he proved that every positive integer can be written as the sum of at most four perfect squares.

Lagrange was born in Turin, Italy, to a family of Italian–French descent and became professor of mathematics at the Royal Artillery School in Turin in 1755 at the age of nineteen. At the invitation of Frederick the Great he succeeded Euler in Berlin in 1766, and remained there until Frederick's death in 1786. He spent the rest of his life in Paris.

Lagrange chaired the committee formed to introduce the metric system to France. He also took a leading role in the reform of university education, becoming professor at the École Normale in Paris in 1795, and at the École Polytechnique in 1797.

His early work contributed to the calculus of variations, which he applied to problems in dynamics. He also worked on the *libration* of the moon; this motion causes the face that the moon presents to the earth to oscillate slightly so that, over time, more than half of the moon's surface can be seen from the earth.

THE THEORY OF FUNCTIONS

Lagrange's two books on functions, *Théorie des Fonctions Analytiques* (1797) and *Leçons sur le Calcul des Fonctions* (1801), attempted to put calculus on to a more secure foundation by taking an algebraic approach rather than one based on a theory of limits. His method was to avoid any mention of tangents, or any use of pictures, and to define functions as infinite "power series." In particular, starting with a function that is written in the form:

$$f(x) = a + bx + cx^2 + dx^3 + \ldots$$

he defined its derivative to be:

$$f'(x) = b + 2cx + 3dx^2 + \ldots$$

Joseph-Louis Lagrange

For example, differentiating the function:

$$\sin x = x - \tfrac{1}{6}x^3 + \tfrac{1}{120}x^5 - \ldots$$

we get $1 - \tfrac{1}{3}x^2 + \tfrac{1}{24}x^4 - \ldots$, which is cos x.

Although this approach to the foundations of the calculus turned out to be unsatisfactory, his abstract treatment of a function was a considerable advance. It essentially gave the first theory of functions of a real variable, with applications to a wide range of problems in geometry and algebra.

MÉCANIQUE ANALYTIQUE

Lagrange's *Mécanique Analytique* (Analytical Mechanics) was his most important work. Published in 1788, just over a century after Newton's *Principia Mathematica*, it took a completely different approach to mechanics. It extended the work of Newton, the Bernoullis, and Euler, and explained how one can generally answer questions about the motion of points and rigid bodies by reducing them to problems in the theory of ordinary and partial differential equations. As its contents page optimistically declared, it presents:

Differential equations, for the solution of all the problems of Dynamics.

In *Mécanique Analytique* Lagrange transformed mechanics into a branch of mathematical analysis, and the geometrical approach that Newton had employed in the *Principia* was totally superseded. Indeed, as Lagrange emphasized in his preface:

One will not find figures in this work. The methods that I expound require neither constructions, nor geometrical or mechanical arguments, but only algebraic operations, subject to a regular and uniform course.

Left: *École Polytechnique students at the tomb of Gaspard Monge*

Solving Polynomial Equations

As we have seen, people have solved quadratic equations since Mesopotamian times, using only arithmetic operations (addition, subtraction, multiplication, and division) and the taking of roots. In the sixteenth century, Italian mathematicians developed similar solutions to cubic equations (of degree 3) and quartic equations (of degree 4). We can solve all of these equations by means of formulas that involve only arithmetic operations and the taking of roots.

But how about equations of degree 5 (or more)? The corresponding search for a general solution or formula for these occupied the finest mathematicians, such as Descartes and Euler, but little progress was made on the problem until Lagrange attempted it, laying the groundwork for the eventual solution.

Lagrange's approach was to consider certain expressions involving the solutions of the equations (such as their sum or product) and to investigate how many different values these expressions can take when the solutions are permuted among themselves; for example, if the solutions of an equation are a, b, and c, and the expression is $ab + c$, then we obtain three different values on permuting the solutions: $ab + c$, $ac + b$, and $bc + a$. Out of such explorations came a result that later became known, in a more general setting, as *Lagrange's theorem for groups.*

It was not until the 1820s that a proof finally emerged of the impossibility of solving the general equation of degree 5 (or more) by arithmetical operations and the taking of roots. This proof relied heavily on the ideas that Lagrange had put forward.

Pierre-Simon Laplace

Pierre-Simon Laplace (1749–1827) was the last leading mathematician of the eighteenth century. He wrote a ground-breaking text on the analytical theory of probability, and is also remembered for the "Laplace transform" of a function and Laplace's equation. His monumental five-volume work on celestial mechanics earned him the title of "the Newton of France."

Laplace was born in Normandy in France. Through the influence of d'Alembert he obtained a teaching position at the École Militaire in Paris, where legend has it that he examined (and passed) Napoleon. In 1790, during the French Revolution, he was appointed as a member of the committee of the Academy of Sciences formed to standardize weights and measures, and was subsequently involved with the organization of the École Normale and École Polytechnique.

THE *MÉCANIQUE CÉLESTE*

Laplace's *Traité de Mécanique Céleste* (Treatise on Celestial Mechanics), published in five volumes (the first two in 1799), consolidated the work of Newton, Clairaut, d'Alembert, Euler, and Lagrange and his own researches. It was accompanied by an essay, *Exposition du Systeme du Monde* (Exposition on the System of the World), where he stated his philosophy of science:

> *If man were restricted to collecting facts the sciences were only a sterile nomenclature and he would never have known the great laws of nature. It is in comparing the*

Pierre-Simon Laplace

> *phenomena with each other, in seeking to grasp their relationships, that he is led to discover these laws…*

Laplace's work considered:

- the gravitational attraction of a spheroid on a particle outside it, and what we now know as *Laplace's equation* for the gravitational potential;
- the motion of the moon;
- the motion of three bodies under mutual gravitational attraction;
- the perturbations of the planets and the stability of the solar system;
- the nebular hypothesis for the formation of the solar system, arising from the contracting and cooling of a large mass of hot rotating gas.

LAPLACE AND NAPOLEON

A well-known story, probably apocryphal, concerns the *Mécanique Céleste*. Summoned by Napoleon to give an account of his recently published book on the solar system, Laplace was asked by the emperor why, unlike Isaac Newton, he had not mentioned God in his treatise. "Sire," replied Laplace, "I had no need of that hypothesis."

> 282   ATTRACTIONS OF SPHEROIDS.   [Méc. Cél.
>
> therefore we shall have
>
> [459]
> Important
> Equation
> for com-
> puting the $$0 = \left(\frac{ddV}{dx^2}\right) + \left(\frac{ddV}{dy^2}\right) + \left(\frac{ddV}{dz^2}\right). \qquad (A)$$
> attrac-
> tions of   This remarkable equation will be of the greatest use to us, in the theory of
> Spheroids
> and the   the figures of the heavenly bodies. We may put it under other forms which
> figures
> of the   are more convenient on several occasions.
> Heavenly
> Bodies.
> [459']

Laplace's equation, from an English translation of Mécanique Céleste

PROBABILITY THEORY

Laplace's *Théorie Analytique des Probabilités* (Analytic Theory of Probability) of 1812 contains Laplace's definition of probability:

The theory of chance consists in the reduction of all events of the same kind to a certain number of equally likely cases that are cases such that we are equally undecided about their existence and in determining the number of cases which are favorable to the event whose probability is sought. The ratio to that of all the cases possible is the measure of this probability, which is thus simply the fraction whose numerator is the number of favorable cases, and whose denominator is the number of all cases possible.

Laplace introduced generating functions for the solution of difference equations and also obtained approximations to binomial distributions. He worked on what is now called "Bayes' theorem," which is relevant when an event can be produced by different causes: if the event happens, what is the probability that it was produced by a particular cause? As an example of his analysis he asked:

Over the period 1745–1770, 251,527 boys and 241,945 girls were born in Paris. Is this evidence that the probability of a male birth is greater than 0.5?

His analysis showed, with extremely high probability, that this is indeed the case.

Laplace's statue in his birthplace of Beaumont-en-Auge, France

Determinism

Laplace believed in determinism, which he explains in the following quotation from the introduction to his non-technical *Essai Philosophique sur les Probabilités* (A Philosophical Essay on Probabilities):

We may regard the present state of the universe as the effect of its past and the cause of its future. An intellect which at a certain moment would know all forces that set nature in motion, and all positions of all items of which nature is composed, if this intellect were also vast enough to submit these data to analysis, it would embrace in a single formula the movements of the greatest bodies of the universe and those of the tiniest atom; for such an intellect nothing would be uncertain and the future just like the past would be present before its eyes.

THE AGE OF REVOLUTIONS

The nineteenth century saw the development of a mathematics profession in which people earned their living from teaching, examining, and researching. The mathematical center of gravity moved from France to Germany, while Latin gave way to national languages for publishing mathematical work. There was also a dramatic increase in the number of textbooks and journals.

Because of this increase in mathematical activity, mathematicians began to (indeed, needed to) specialize. While one would use the term *mathematician* in the eighteenth century, one now had *analysts, algebraists, geometers, number theorists, logicians,* and *applied mathematicians.* This need for specialization was avoided only by the very greatest: Gauss, Hamilton, Riemann, and Klein.

In each discipline there was a revolution (as well as an evolution) in the depth, extent, and even the very existence of the discipline. But each discipline experienced a movement toward an increasingly abstract style, with an increased emphasis on putting mathematics on a sound and rigorous basis and examining its foundations.

We illustrate this here by considering the revolutions in three areas—analysis, algebra, and geometry.

The University of Göttingen, where Gauss, Riemann, and Klein worked.

FROM CALCULUS TO ANALYSIS

In the 1820s, Augustin-Louis Cauchy, the most prolific mathematician of the century, rigorized the calculus by basing it on the concept of a *limit.* He then used this idea to develop the areas of real and complex analysis. This increase in rigor necessitated the formulation of a foolproof definition of the real numbers—which in turn led to a study of infinite sets by Georg Cantor and others.

Joseph Fourier's work on heat conduction also gave rise to infinite processes—in this case, infinite series—thereby stimulating Bernhard Riemann in his work on integration. Analytical techniques came to be applied to a wide range of problems—in electricity and magnetism by William Thomson (Lord Kelvin) and James Clerk Maxwell, in hydrodynamics by George Gabriel Stokes, and in probability and number theory by Pafnuty Chebyshev.

FROM EQUATIONS TO STRUCTURES

Algebra also changed dramatically throughout the nineteenth century. In 1800 the subject was about solving equations, but by 1900 it had become the study of mathematical structures—sets of elements that are combined according to specified rules, called *axioms.*

At the beginning of the century, Gauss laid down the basics of number theory and introduced modular arithmetic, an early example of a new algebraic structure called a *group.*

A long–standing problem had to do with finding a general method for solving polynomial equations of degree 5 or more, using only arithmetical operations and the taking of roots.

Niels Abel showed that there can be no such general solution, and Évariste Galois developed his ideas by examining groups of permutations of the roots of an equation.

The mystique concerning complex numbers was at last removed by William Rowan Hamilton, who defined them as pairs of real numbers with certain operations. Other algebraic structures were discovered: Hamilton introduced the algebra of quaternions, George Boole created an algebra for use in logic and probability, and Cayley studied the algebra of rectangular arrays of symbols, called *matrices*.

FROM ONE TO MANY GEOMETRIES

Over the space of one hundred years the study of geometry was completely transformed. In 1800 the only "true" geometry had been Euclidean geometry, although there were some scattered results on spherical and projective geometry. By the end of the century, infinitely many geometries were known, while geometry had

Above: *Revolutions did not happen only in mathematics: this is a miners' riot that took place in Belgium, 1868.*

become closely linked to group theory and placed on a more rigorous foundation.

Gauss studied surfaces and their curvature, finding a relationship between curvature and the sum of the angles of a triangle on the surface. This turned out to be related to the investigations into the parallel postulate in Euclidean geometry. Nikolai Lobachevsky and János Bolyai independently developed non-Euclidean geometry, in which the parallel postulate does not hold.

It took time, however, for the ideas on non-Euclidean geometry to become absorbed, and it was the mid-century work of Riemann that showed the importance of the new ideas and extended the work of Gauss. Through such abstract techniques, geometry was also moving out of two and three dimensions and into higher ones. Later, Felix Klein used groups to examine and classify different types of geometry.

Carl Friedrich Gauss

Carl Friedrich Gauss (1777–1855) was one of the greatest mathematicians of all time. He made significant contributions to a wide variety of fields, including astronomy, geodesy, optics, statistics, differential geometry, and magnetism. He presented the first satisfactory proof of the fundamental theorem of algebra and the first systematic study of the convergence of series. In number theory he introduced congruences and discovered when a regular polygon can be constructed with an unmarked ruler and pair of compasses. Although he claimed to have discovered a "non-Euclidean geometry," he published nothing on it.

Gauss was born in the Duchy of Brunswick, now in Germany. A child prodigy, he reputedly summed all the integers from 1 to 100 by spotting that the total of 5,050 arises from 50 pairs of numbers, with each pair summing to 101:

$$101 = 1 + 100 = 2 + 99 = \ldots = 50 + 51$$

He went to Göttingen University in 1795, later returning to Brunswick, until he was appointed director of the Göttingen Observatory in 1807. He remained there for the rest of his life.

Gauss's *Disquisitiones Arithmeticae* (Discourses in Arithmetic) was published in 1801 when he was only twenty-four. It was his most famous work, earning him the title of the "Prince of Mathematics." His view of number theory is captured in a famous quotation that is attributed to him:

Mathematics is the queen of the sciences, and number theory is the queen of mathematics.

CONSTRUCTING POLYGONS

In his teenage years Gauss became interested in the construction of regular polygons, using only an unmarked ruler and a pair of compasses. In the first proposition of Euclid's *Elements* we learn how to construct an equilateral triangle, and the *Elements* also contains constructions for a square and a regular pentagon.

We can also start with a regular *n*-sided polygon and construct a 2*n*-sided polygon. For example, from an equilateral triangle we can construct regular polygons with 6, 12, and 24

Left: *Gauss at his astronomical observatory in Göttingen*

sides, while a square gives polygons with 8, 16, and 32 sides, and a regular pentagon gives those with 10, 20, and 40 sides. But no one can construct a regular polygon with 7 or 9 sides—so which regular polygons are constructible?

Gauss approached this question by first describing a complicated geometrical method for constructing a regular 17-sided polygon. He then analyzed the general case, and came up with a surprising answer, involving the Fermat primes: the known ones are 3, 5, 17, 257, and 65,537. He found that:

> *A regular n-sided polygon can be constructed if and only if n can be obtained by multiplying any number of different Fermat primes and then doubling as often as we wish.*

MODULAR ARITHMETIC

At the beginning of *Disquisitiones Arithmeticae* Gauss laid the foundations of number theory as a discipline with its own techniques and methods. To do so, he introduced modular arithmetic and congruences, a topic that exemplifies the rising abstraction of nineteenth-century mathematics.

For any positive integer n, two numbers a and b are said to be congruent *modulo n* if n divides $a - b$; n is called the *modulus* and we write $a \equiv b$ mod n: so $37 \equiv 7$ mod 10, since 10 divides $37 - 7$. So if $n = 10$, we are dealing with the remainders 0, 1, 2, ... , 9 obtained after division by 10, because every integer is congruent mod 10 to just one of these.

Using his congruences, Gauss proved a famous result of Euler, known as the quadratic reciprocity theorem:

> *If p and q are odd prime numbers, then $x^2 \equiv p$ mod q has a solution if, and only if, $x^2 \equiv q$ mod p does, except when $p \equiv 3$ mod 4 and $q \equiv 3$ mod 4.*

ASTRONOMY AND STATISTICS

Also in 1801, the year of the *Disquisitiones Arithmeticae*, Gauss established himself as one of Europe's leading astronomers. On the first day of the century, Giuseppe Piazzi discovered the asteroid Ceres, the first new object discovered

The Fundamental Theorem of Algebra

The subject of Gauss's doctoral thesis, this theorem states that:

Every polynomial factorizes completely into linear and quadratic factors.

It follows that every polynomial equation of degree n has n complex solutions.

in the solar system since William Herschel had found Uranus twenty years earlier. Piazzi was able to observe it for only forty-two days before it disappeared behind the sun. But where would it reappear? Many astronomers gave their predictions, but only Gauss's was correct, thereby causing great excitement.

In his investigation of the orbit of Ceres, Gauss developed numerical and statistical techniques that would have lasting importance. In particular was his work on *the method of least squares*, which deals with the effect of errors of measurement. In this, he assumed that the errors in the measurements were distributed in a way that is now known as the *Gaussian* or *normal distribution*.

A digitally generated image of Ceres

Augustin-Louis Cauchy

As we have seen, the foundations of the calculus were found to be shaky and d'Alembert and others attempted to rescue them. The difficulties were overcome by Augustin-Louis Cauchy (1789–1857), who was the leading mathematician in France and the most important analyst of the early nineteenth century. In the 1820s he transformed the subject by formalizing the concepts of limit, continuity, derivative, and integral. In addition, he helped to develop the algebraic idea of a "group" and almost single-handedly created the subject of complex analysis.

After training as a civil engineer, Cauchy went to Cherbourg where he worked on designs for the harbor and the fortifications. His first mathematical papers were on polyhedra and algebra. He was soon elected to the Academy of Sciences and moved to Paris, where he lectured at the École Polytechnique.

BOLZANO

In 1817, in his home city of Prague, a Catholic priest named Bernard Bolzano published a pamphlet snappily entitled *A Purely Analytic Proof of the Theorem that, Between any Two Values that give Results of Opposite Sign Lies at least One Real Root of the Equation.* This result is now known as the *Intermediate value theorem*, and tells us that:

A continuous graph that is below the x-axis at one place and above it at another must cross the x-axis at some point in between.

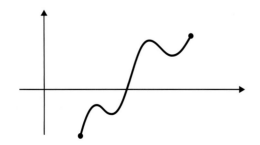

Although this result may seem obvious, Bolzano's pamphlet contained its first rigorous proof.

Intuitively, a graph is "continuous" if it has no gaps, but Bolzano found it necessary to formalize this idea:

A function f(x) varies continuously for all values of x in a certain interval if, for any x in that interval, the difference f(x + ω) − f(x) can be made smaller than any given quantity by insisting ω that be taken as small as we please.

For example, if $f(x) = x^2$ between 0 to 1, then, for any value of x in this range,

$$f(x + \omega) - f(x) = (x + \omega)^2 - x^2 = \omega (2x + \omega)$$

which can be made as small as we please by choosing ω to be small enough. So $f(x) = x^2$ is continuous on this interval.

However, Bolzano's work never had the credit it deserved, as Prague was situated far from the centers of mathematical activity.

CAUCHY'S *COURS D'ANALYSE*

Meanwhile, much progress was being made in Paris. In 1821, Cauchy produced a ground-breaking book entitled *Cours d'Analyse* (Course of Analysis) in which he formalized the idea of a limit:

Cauchy's Complex Analysis

We have seen how Leibniz defined the integral $\int_a^b f(x)\,dx$ of a function f as a "sum of lines"—we can think of this informally as the result of "adding up all the values of $f(x)$" as x travels from a to b.

In the late 1820s Cauchy explained how this idea can be extended to complex numbers. If $f(z)$ is a function of a complex variable z (such as $f(z) = z^2$), and if P is a curve in the complex plane, then we can analogously define $\int_P f(z)\,dz$ as the result of "adding up all the values of $f(z)$" as z travels along the curve P.

Cauchy proved many spectacular results concerning these complex integrals. The most powerful of these results involves integrating functions that are differentiable around closed curves (curves whose ends coincide, such as those shown). Known as *Cauchy's theorem*, it tells us that $\int_P f(z)\,dz = 0$ whenever f is differentiable and P is a closed curve.

Some closed paths

Furthermore, *Cauchy's integral formula* states that if a is any point inside the closed curve P, then:

$$f(a) = 1/(2\pi i) \int_P f(z) / (z - a)\,dz$$

This tells us that we can find the value of $f(a)$ at any point a inside P from the values of $f(z)$ at all points z on P. It is rather like calculating the temperature at an inland place like Birmingham when we are told the temperatures at all points along the British coastline—a remarkable result.

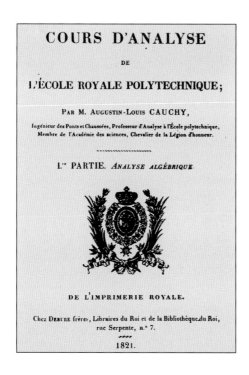

When the values successively attributed to the same variable approach a fixed value indefinitely, in such a way as to end up by differing from it as little as we could wish, this last value is called the limit of all the others.

For example, $f(x) = (\sin x)/x$ is not defined when $x = 0$ (since 0/0 is meaningless), but as x approaches the value 0, $f(x)$ approaches the value 1, so 1 is the limit in this case.

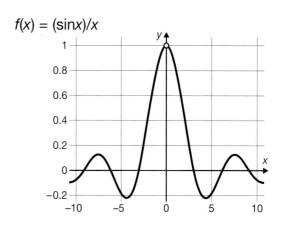

$f(x) = (\sin x)/x$

Using this definition, Cauchy was able to transform the whole subject. He gave rigorous explanations of what it means to say that a graph is *continuous* (no gaps) and smooth (no corners), and also gave rigorous presentations of the two fundamental concepts of the calculus, *differentiation* and *integration*.

Fourier and Poisson

Joseph Fourier (1768–1830) worked on what are now known as Fourier series: *this led to many of the most important mathematical discoveries of the nineteenth century, and had major applications in mathematical physics. Siméon Denis Poisson (1781–1840) has his name attached to* Poisson's equation *in potential theory and the* Poisson distribution *in probability theory.*

Fourier was born in Auxerre in France, and in 1797 succeeded Lagrange in the chair of analysis and mechanics at the École Polytechnique, leaving the following year with Gaspard Monge to join Napoleon's invasion of Egypt as a scientific adviser. On his return he was appointed by Napoleon to an administrative position at Grenoble in south-eastern France, organizing the draining of the swamps of Bourgoin and supervising the building of the road from Grenoble to Turin. In his spare time he carried out his important mathematical research on the conduction of heat.

THE CONDUCTION OF HEAT

In his 1822 *Théorie Analytique de la Chaleur* (Analytic Theory of Heat), Fourier wrote:

> *Fundamental causes are not known to us; but they are subject to simple and constant laws, which one can discover by observation and whose study is the object of natural philosophy.*

Fourier began his investigations into heat by obtaining a partial differential equation for the equilibrium temperature distribution in a rectangular region, where the temperatures at the boundaries are kept constant. This led to his deriving a representation of a *square wave* in terms, not of a power series, but of the infinite trigonometric series:

$$\cos u - \tfrac{1}{3}\cos 3u + \tfrac{1}{5}\cos 5u - \tfrac{1}{7}\cos 7u + \ldots$$

which equals 0 when $u = \pi/2$,
$\pi/4$ when u lies between $-\pi/2$ and $\pi/2$,
and $-\pi/4$ when u lies between $\pi/2$ and $3\pi/2$.

Joseph Fourier

He wrote about this surprising outcome:

> *As these results appear to depart from the ordinary consequences of the calculus, it is necessary to examine them with care, and to interpret them in their true sense.*

Fourier then considered the more general question of which functions can be represented by *Fourier series*, first defining what he meant by a function:

> *In general, a function f(x) represents a succession of values or ordinates each of which is arbitrary. An infinity of values being given to the abscissa x, there is an equal number of ordinates f(x). ... We do not*

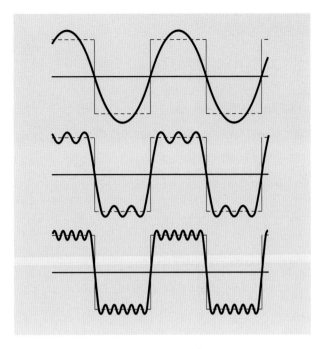

Approximating a square wave by a Fourier series

> *suppose these ordinates to be subject to a common law: they succeed each other in any manner whatsoever, and each of them is given as if it were a single quantity.*

Fourier did not consider functions as general as those described in his definition, but rather as those that are given by different rules over different sections where they are defined. He also derived formulas (involving integrals) for the coefficients in the *Fourier series* of the function.

The question of what conditions should be imposed on a function so as to ensure that its *Fourier series* does indeed converge to the original function generated much new activity, by Abel and Riemann among others.

SIMÉON DENIS POISSON

Poisson was born in Pithiviers in north-central France and quickly achieved academic success, occupying many educational positions—in particular, succeeding Fourier in 1806 at the École Polytechnique after Napoleon had sent Fourier to Grenoble. He published many mathematical works and, according to François Arago, frequently said:

> *Life is good for only two things, discovering mathematics and teaching mathematics.*

Poisson carried out major work on electricity, magnetism, and elasticity, obtaining (for example) a partial differential equation giving the electric potential for a given distribution of the electric charges. In 1812 he won the French Academy's Grand Prix, where the topic was:

> *To determine by calculation and to confirm by experiment the manner in which electricity is distributed at the surface of electrical bodies considered either in isolation or in the presence of each other—for example, at the surface of two electrified spheres in the presence of each other.*

In his 1838 *Recherches sur la Probabilité des Jugements en Matière Criminelle et en Matière Civile* (Researches on the Probability of Judgments in Criminal and Civil Matters), he introduced what is now known as the *Poisson distribution*. This important distribution gives the probabilities of how many times an event occurs in an interval of time or a region of space. It makes certain assumptions that the events occur independently, and about how many occur in a short interval of time or a small region of space. He also introduced the term *law of large numbers*.

Siméon Denis Poisson

Abel and Galois

The tragic stories of Niels Henrik Abel (1802–29) and Évariste Galois (1811–32) are depressingly similar. Both found it difficult to get their results accepted, and although both made major advances in the theory of equations—Abel proved that no general solution can exist for polynomial equations of degree 5 or more, while Galois determined when such equations can be solved—both died young, Abel from tuberculosis and Galois after being wounded in a duel.

Earlier we saw that polynomial equations of degrees 2, 3, and 4 had been solved with only arithmetic operations and the taking of roots, but that no one had been able to do the same for general equations of higher degrees. We also saw Lagrange's new approach to such problems, where he counted the number of different expressions that one can obtain by permuting the solutions of the given equation.

NIELS HENRIK ABEL

Growing up in Norway, Abel was desperate to study in the main centers of mathematical life in France and Germany, and was eventually able to obtain a stipend that enabled him to spend time in Paris and Berlin.

In Germany he met Leopold Crelle and published many papers in the early issues of Crelle's new journal, thereby helping it to become the leading German mathematical periodical of the nineteenth century; among these papers was the one that contained his proof of the impossibility for solving the general equation of degree 5 or more. He also obtained fundamental results on other topics (the convergence of series, elliptic functions, and "Abelian integrals"), many of which appeared in his "Paris memoir" of 1826.

The story of Abel's attempts to be recognized by the mathematical community, and of his lack of success in securing an academic post, is a sorry one. For a time, his Paris memoir was lost. He then returned to Norway where he contracted tuberculosis and died aged only twenty-six. Two days later, a letter arrived at his home, informing him that his memoir had been found and offering him a prestigious professorship in Berlin.

ÉVARISTE GALOIS

The work of Lagrange and Abel on the unsolvability of the general quintic equation was developed by the brilliant Évariste Galois, who determined criteria (in terms of an object now called the *Galois group*) for deciding *which* polynomial equations can be solved by arithmetical operations and the taking of roots. His work ultimately led to whole new areas of algebra, now known as group theory and *Galois theory*.

Born in France, Galois's teenage years were traumatic. He failed his entrance examination for the École Polytechnique. A manuscript that he sent to the French Academy of Sciences was mislaid, and another

Niels Henrik Abel

Évariste Galois

was rejected for being obscure; and his father committed suicide.

A republican firebrand who became involved with political activities following the July Revolution of 1830, Galois threatened the life of King Louis-Philippe, but was acquitted. A month later he was discovered carrying weapons and wearing the uniform of the banned artillery guard, whereupon he was thrown into jail.

Galois spent the night before his duel frantically scribbling a letter to his friend August Chevalier, summarizing his results and requesting Chevalier to show them to Gauss and Jacobi. But it was to be several years before anyone appreciated what they meant, and what a genius the world had lost.

APPLYING 19TH-CENTURY ALGEBRA

As we have seen, the Greeks were fascinated by geometrical constructions. Using only an unmarked ruler and a pair of compasses, they bisected angles, trisected line segments, and constructed squares with the same area as a given polygon. But there were three types of construction that defeated them:

DOUBLING A CUBE
Given a cube, construct another cube with twice the volume.

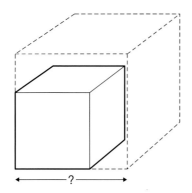

TRISECTING AN ANGLE
Given any angle, divide it into three equal parts.

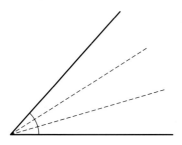

SQUARING THE CIRCLE
Given any circle, construct a square with the same area.

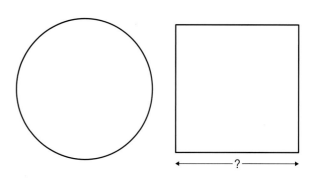

These all date from the fourth century BCE, and for the next two millennia valid constructions were sought, without success.

Starting with a line of length 1, we can mark out its multiples, and then construct lines of any lengths that are rational numbers (fractions). By intersecting these lines with circles, and intersecting circles with other circles, we find that:

We can construct any lengths involving basic arithmetic operations and the successive taking of square roots, but no other lengths.

Doubling a cube
If the first cube has side 1, then the doubled cube has side $\sqrt[3]{2}$, which is a cube root and so cannot be constructed.

Trisecting an angle
If we try to trisect an angle of 60°, we find that $x = \cos 20°$ satisfies the equation $8x^3 - 6x - 1 = 0$, whose solutions involve cube roots that cannot be constructed.

Squaring the circle
This involves π, which also cannot be constructed.

Thus, once nineteenth-century algebraists had proved that none of the lengths $\sqrt[3]{2}$, cos 20°, and π can be constructed, it followed that:

All three types of construction are impossible.

Bolyai and Lobachevsky

As we have seen, Euclid's Elements *is built on five self-evident truths, called* postulates. *Four of these are straightforward, but the fifth is different in style. For two thousand years people tried to deduce it from the other four, but no one could do so. This is because there are "non-Euclidean" geometries that satisfy the first four postulates, but not the fifth. Their existence was first published around 1830 by the Transylvanian János Bolyai (1802–60) and the Russian Nikolai Lobachevsky (1792–1856).*

Over the centuries, many tried to prove the fifth postulate by deducing it from other results in Euclid's *Elements* to which it is equivalent. Two of these were the "parallel postulate":

> *Given any line L and any point P that does not lie on this line, there is exactly one line, parallel to L, that passes through P*

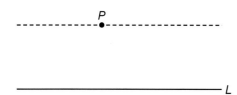

and the "angle-sum theorem for rectangles":

> *The angles of any rectangle add up to 360°.*

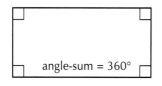
angle-sum = 360°

If one can deduce either of these from the first four postulates, then the fifth postulate must also be true.

SACCHERI'S ATTEMPT

The first really significant advance was in 1733, in *Euclides ab Omni Naevo Vindicatus* (Euclid Vindicated from Every Flaw), by the Italian geometer Gerolamo Saccheri. His approach was to consider geometries in which the fifth postulate is not assumed, and derive a contradiction.

In order to do so, Saccheri attempted to prove that rectangles whose angle-sum is not equal to 360° cannot exist. It would then follow that the angle-sum is always 360° and that the fifth postulate is true.

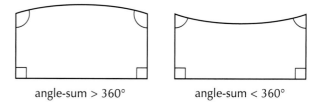
angle-sum > 360°   angle-sum < 360°

Saccheri's first attempts were successful. He proved that if the angle-sum is greater than 360°, then the parallel postulate can be proved both true and false—as Saccheri remarked:

> *It is absolutely false, because it destroys itself.*

This contradiction shows that no geometry can have this property.

He then tried to repeat the process for a rectangle with angle-sum less than 360°, claiming that:

> *The hypothesis of the acute angle is absolutely false, because it is repugnant to the nature of straight lines.*

But here his argument contained an error.

If Saccheri *had* been successful in this case, then he would have proved that the sum of the angles in every rectangle must be 360°. It would then follow that the fifth postulate can indeed be deduced from the other postulates.

NON-EUCLIDEAN GEOMETRIES

Saccheri's approach was proved wrong in spectacular fashion. Around 1830, Bolyai and Lobachevsky independently both constructed a new type of geometry in which:

The angles of any rectangle add up to less than 360°.

In their geometry the first four of Euclid's postulates still hold, but not the fifth one.

This Bolyai–Lobachevsky geometry has some very strange features:

Given any line L and any point P that does not lie on this line, there are infinitely many lines, parallel to L, that pass through P.

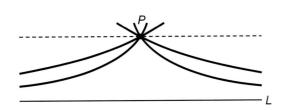

Moreover, *if two triangles are similar* (they have the same angles), *then they must also be congruent* (they have the same size)—which is also not true in Euclidean geometry.

Both Bolyai and Lobachevsky were unsuccessful in getting their work widely known, and they enjoyed little of the credit due to them for their remarkable discovery. It was not until after their deaths that their geometries were fully understood.

THE CONTRIBUTION OF GAUSS

The non-Euclidean geometries of Bolyai and Lobachevsky were considered very controversial, as they were seen not to correspond to the world

Left: *Nikolai Lobachevsky*

we live in. Some years earlier, Gauss had been thinking along similar lines:

I am becoming more and more convinced that the necessity of our [Euclidean] geometry cannot be proved … Perhaps in another life we will be able to obtain insight into the nature of space, which is now unattainable.

However, he was unwilling to publish his startling predictions, fearing "the howl of the Boeotians" if he did so; the Boeotians were ancient Greeks who were resistant to change.

János's father, Farkas Bolyai, had also worked on the parallel postulate and earnestly tried to dissuade his son from doing so:

You must not attempt this approach to parallels. I know its way to its very end. I have traversed this bottomless night, which extinguished all light and joy of my life … I have traveled past all reefs of this infernal Dead Sea and have always come back with broken mast and torn sail.

But the son persisted, and when Farkas Bolyai informed his old friend Gauss of his son's success, Gauss accepted the results but claimed them as his own:

If I commenced by saying that I am unable to praise this work, you would certainly be surprised for a moment. But I cannot say otherwise. To praise it would be to praise myself. Indeed the whole contents of the work, the path taken by your son, the results to which he is led, coincide almost entirely with my meditations, which have occupied my mind partly for the last thirty or thirty-five years.

János Bolyai never forgave Gauss for this.

Babbage and Lovelace

The central figure of nineteenth-century computing was Charles Babbage (1791–1871), who may be said to have pioneered the modern computer age with his "difference engines" and his "analytical engine," although his influence on subsequent generations is hard to assess. Ada, Countess of Lovelace (1816–52), daughter of Lord Byron and a close friend of Babbage, produced a perceptive and clear commentary on the powers and potential of the analytical engine; this was essentially an introduction to what we now call programing.

THE DIFFERENCE ENGINE

Charles Babbage and John Herschel were asked by the Royal Astronomical Society to produce new astronomical tables. It was this that caused Babbage to design his calculating machine.

He wanted to mechanize the calculation of a formula such as $x^2 + x + 41$, for different values of x—this was his illustrative example.

The core of his idea can be seen in the following table. In the second column are the values of this expression for $x = 0, 1, 2, \dots 7$, in the third column are the differences between successive terms of the second (the *first differences*), and in the fourth column are the differences between successive terms of the third column (the *second differences*); here, the second differences are all the same.

x	$x^2 + x + 41$	*first differences*	*second differences*
0	41		
		2	
1	43		2
		4	
2	47		2
		6	
3	53		2
		8	
4	61		2
		10	
5	71		2
		12	
6	83		2
		14	
7	97		

Note that we can reconstruct the values of the function in a steplike fashion from the shaded region containing the first term (41), the initial first difference (2), and the constant second differences (2).

This technique can be applied to any polynomial function, because continuing to take differences eventually yields constant values. Also many functions of interest which are not polynomials (like *sin*, *cos*, and *log*) can be approximated by polynomials.

The construction of the difference engine ran into engineering, financial, and political difficulties, and construction ended in 1833.

A portion of the 1832 difference engine: it was to have the feature of being able to print its results, as more errors arose in printing and proof-reading than in the original calculations.

Charles Babbage

THE ANALYTICAL ENGINE

Babbage wondered whether his difference engine could be made to act upon the results of its own calculations, or as he put it:

The engine eating its own tail.

With this in mind, he designed a new engine, basing its control system on the punched cards used by Jacquard for his automatic loom.

The design for his analytical engine allowed for inputting numbers and holding them in a *store*. The instructions for the operations to be performed on the numbers would be input separately. These operations would be performed in a part of the computer, called the *mill*, and the results would be returned to the store and printed, or used as input for a further calculation, depending on the control instructions. Importantly, the operations to be performed could be made to depend on the result of an earlier calculation.

Ada, Countess of Lovelace, was encouraged in her interest in mathematics by Mary Somerville and Augustus De Morgan.

In her writings on the analytical engine, she described what it could do and how it could be instructed, and gave what is considered to be the first computer program. As she wrote:

The distinctive characteristic of the Analytical Engine ... is the introduction into it of the principle which Jacquard devised for regulating, by means of punched cards, the most complicated patterns in the fabrication of brocaded stuffs. It is in this that the distinction between the two engines lies. Nothing of the sort exists in the Difference Engine. We may say most aptly that the Analytical Engine weaves algebraical patterns just as the Jacquard loom weaves flowers and leaves.

Although the analytical engine was never built, modern scholarship is of the view that if it had been constructed, it would have worked as Babbage intended. The name ADA is now given to a programing language developed for the United States Department of Defense.

Ada, Countess of Lovelace

Florence Nightingale

Florence Nightingale (1820–1910), the "lady with the lamp" who saved lives during the Crimean War, was also a fine statistician who collected and analyzed mortality data from the Crimea and displayed them on her "polar diagrams," a forerunner of the pie chart. Her work was strongly influenced by that of the Belgian statistician Adolphe Quetelet.

Florence Nightingale showed an early interest in mathematics—at the age of nine she was displaying data in tabular form, and by the age of twenty she was receiving tuition in mathematics, possibly from James Joseph Sylvester.

Nightingale regarded statistics as "the most important science in the world" and used statistical methods to support her efforts at administrative and social reform. She was the first woman to be elected a Fellow of the Royal Statistical Society and an honorary foreign member of the American Statistical Association.

STATISTICAL INFLUENCE

By 1852 Nightingale had established a reputation as an effective administrator and project manager. Her work on the professionalization of nursing led to her accepting the position of "Superintendent of the female nursing establishment in the English General Military Hospitals in Turkey" for the British troops fighting in the Crimean war. She arrived in 1854 and was appalled at what she found there. In attempting to change attitudes and practices she made use of pictorial diagrams for statistical information, developing her *polar area graphs*.

The graphs have twelve sectors, one for each month, and reveal changes over the year in the deaths from wounds obtained in battle, from diseases, and from other causes. They showed dramatically the extent of the needless deaths among the soldiers during the Crimean war, and were used to persuade medical and other

Below: *Florence Nightingale's polar area graph*

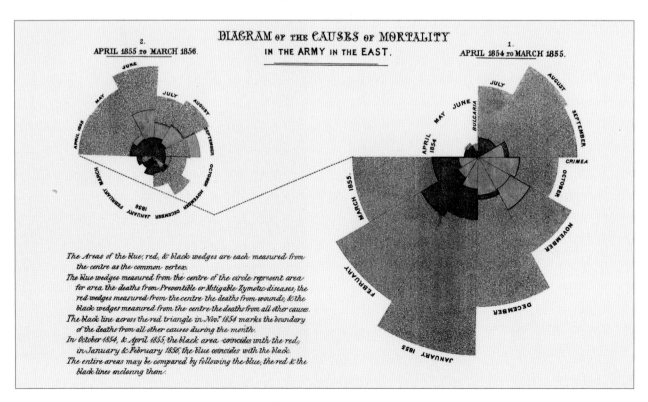

DIAGRAM of the CAUSES of MORTALITY IN THE ARMY IN THE EAST.

2. APRIL 1855 to MARCH 1856.

1. APRIL 1854 to MARCH 1855.

The Areas of the blue, red, & black wedges are each measured from the centre as the common vertex.

The blue wedges measured from the centre of the circle represent area for area the deaths from Preventible or Mitigable Zymotic diseases, the red wedges measured from the centre the deaths from wounds, & the black wedges measured from the centre the deaths from all other causes.

The black line across the red triangle in Nov.ʳ 1854 marks the boundary of the deaths from all other causes during the month.

In October 1854, & April 1855, the black area coincides with the red; in January & February 1856, the blue coincides with the black.

The entire areas may be compared by following the blue, the red & the black lines enclosing them.

professionals that deaths could be prevented if sanitary and other reforms were made.

On her return to London in 1858, she continued to use statistics to inform and influence public health policy. She urged the collection of the same data, across different hospitals, of:

- the number of patients in hospital,
- the type of treatment, broken down by age, sex, and disease,
- the length of stay in hospital,
- the recovery rate of patients.

She argued for the inclusion in the 1861 census of questions on the number of sick people in a household, and on the standard of housing, as she realized the important relationship between health and housing. In another initiative she attempted to educate members of the government in the usefulness of statistics, and influence the future by establishing the teaching of the subject in the universities.

For Nightingale the collection of data was only the beginning. Her subsequent analysis and interpretation was crucial and led to medical and social improvements and political reform, all with the aim of saving lives.

Florence Nightingale

Adolphe Quetelet

Above: *Adolphe Quetelet*

Right: *Quetelet's curve, showing the distribution of some of his results*

Quetelet was supervisor of statistics for Belgium, pioneering techniques for taking the national census. His desire to find the statistical characteristics of an "average man" led to his compiling the chest measurements of 5,732 Scottish soldiers and observing that the results were arranged around a mean of 40 inches, according to the normal (or Gaussian) distribution. Taken with some earlier studies of life annuity payments by Edmond Halley and others, Quetelet's investigations helped to lay the foundations of modern actuarial science.

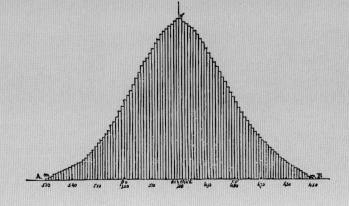

Bernhard Riemann

In many areas the work of Bernhard Riemann (1826–66) had as much influence as that of any other nineteenth-century mathematician. With his remarkable combination of geometrical reasoning and physical insight, he developed the general theory of functions of a complex variable, using his "Riemann surfaces" as a bridge between analysis and geometry, while developing the theory of integration and the convergence of series. In another direction, he obtained a remarkable generalization of the idea of "geometry," both Euclidean and non-Euclidean; years later, one of his geometries proved to be the natural setting for Einstein's theory of relativity. In number theory he left us with what many consider to be the most important unsolved problem in mathematics.

Riemann was born in Breselenz in Northern Germany and studied at the University of Göttingen, obtaining his doctorate there in 1851. Gauss wrote that Riemann's thesis exhibited:

> *A creative, active, truly mathematical mind, and of a gloriously fertile originality.*

In 1859, Riemann was appointed to Gauss's former position as professor of mathematics at Göttingen, succeeding the algebraist and number-theorist Lejeune Dirichlet. Riemann held

Bernhard Riemann

this position for seven years, until his early death at the age of forty.

RIEMANN'S GEOMETRY

Riemann's work in complex analysis was the true beginning of topology, the area of geometry concerned with those properties of space that are unchanged by continuous deformation.

Riemann was also interested in the geometry of higher dimensions. Although we cannot visualize dimensions larger than three, we can still investigate them mathematically. Any point in the two-dimensional plane can be represented by two coordinates (a, b), and similarly we can represent any point in three-dimensional space by three coordinates (a, b, c).

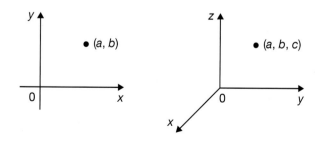

Analogously, we can represent any point in four-dimensional space by four coordinates (a, b, c, d), and similarly for five, six, and higher dimensions. We can then work out lengths and angles in these higher dimensions—just as before, but less easy to visualize.

The Riemann Hypothesis

We have seen that Euler solved one of the big challenges of the early eighteenth century (the *Basel problem*) by proving that:

$$1 + (½)^2 + (⅓)^2 + (¼)^2 + (⅕)^2 + \ldots = \pi^2/6$$

He also proved that:

$$1 + (½)^4 + (⅓)^4 + (¼)^4 + (⅕)^4 + \ldots = \pi^4/90$$
$$1 + (½)^6 + (⅓)^6 + (¼)^6 + (⅕)^6 + \ldots = \pi^6/945$$

and so on, up to the 26th powers. Generalizing this idea, he defined the *zeta function* $\zeta(k)$ by:

$$\zeta(k) = 1 + (½)^k + (⅓)^k + (¼)^k + (⅕)^k + \ldots$$

so $\zeta(2) = \pi^2/6$, $\zeta(4) = \pi^4/90$, $\zeta(6) = \pi^6/945$, etc.

It turns out that $\zeta(k)$ is defined for every real number $k > 1$. However, as we saw earlier, the harmonic series $1 + ½ + ⅓ + ¼ + ⅕ + \ldots$ has no finite sum, so $\zeta(1)$ is not defined.

Can we define the zeta function for other numbers, such as 0 or –4 or even the complex number ½ + 3*i*? In 1859, Riemann found a way of doing so for every real or complex number (except 1), and the function is now known as the *Riemann zeta function*.

It turns out that major problems involving prime numbers are related to the *zeros of the zeta function*—the solutions of the equation $\zeta(z) = 0$ in the complex plane. It also turns out that the zeta function has zeros at –2, –4, –6, –8, … , and that all other zeros lie within a vertical strip between 0 and 1, called the *critical strip*. Moreover, all the *known* zeros in the critical strip (several billion of them, in fact!) occur at points of the form ½ + *ki*, for some number *k*, and so they lie on a vertical line known as the *critical line*. So the question arises: *do all the zeros in the critical strip lie on this line?* That's the big question that we now call the *Riemann hypothesis*. It is generally believed to be true, but no one has been able to prove it, even after 150 years.

Riemann also studied the way that surfaces can "curve" inward or outward (like a globe or a cooling tower) and proposed generalized ideas of distance for such surfaces, not only in three dimensions, but also for their higher-dimensional analogs (called *manifolds*). By disregarding the surrounding higher-dimensional space, he could study manifolds in their own right and measure distances on them. Arising from this work, he was able to describe *infinitely many* different geometries, each one equally valid, and each one a candidate for the physical space we live in.

FUNCTIONS AND SERIES

Other pioneering areas of research arose from Riemann's investigations into which functions can be represented by their *Fourier series*. This developed the theory of functions of a real variable, raised a problem that inspired Cantor in his famous theory of sets, and led to his definition of the *Riemann integral*.

Part of this investigation was his *rearrangement theorem*, which illustrates the subtlety needed for a study of infinite series. Dirichlet had shown that an infinite series can converge to different answers when we alter the order in which the terms are combined. For example, if we take the series:

$$1 - ½ + ⅓ - ¼ + ⅕ - ⅙ + ⅐ - \ldots = \log_e 2$$

and rearrange it so that two positive terms are followed by a negative term, then the resulting series has a different sum:

$$(1 + ⅓) - ½ + (⅕ + ⅐) - ¼ + \ldots = \tfrac{3}{2}\log_e 2$$

Riemann developed this idea by showing that such an infinite series can be rearranged to give any answer whatsoever!

Georg Cantor

The creation of modern set theory is due to Georg Cantor (1845–1918). He established the importance of one-to-one correspondences between sets and founded the theory of transfinite numbers, showing, in particular, that infinities can have different sizes. This work arose from his various investigations into the convergence of Fourier series *and into whether just one trigonometrical series can represent a given function.*

Cantor was born in St Petersburg and began his university studies at the Polytechnic in Zürich, Switzerland, moving after a year to the more prestigious Berlin University where he took his doctorate. In 1869 he became a lecturer at the University of Halle, being promoted to professor ten years later. Although he had always hoped to obtain a position in Berlin, he remained in Halle for the rest of his life, teaching there for many years before succumbing to severe mental illness.

Georg Cantor

SET THEORY

Cantor introduced his theory of sets in a number of papers dating from 1874. For him, a set was:

> *any collection into a whole M of definite and separate objects m of our intuition or of our thought.*

The objects *m* making up the set are called its *elements*. With this very abstract definition, a set could have as elements many different kinds of things, such as the people in the world, the positive integers, or the real numbers. A *subset* of a set *B* is a set whose elements are also elements of *B*.

Two sets *A* and *B* are said to be *equivalent*—we can think of this as meaning that they have the same size—if we can match them up exactly; that is, there is a one-to-one correspondence between the elements of *A* and those of *B*. If the sets *A* and *B* are finite then they must have the same number of elements, but if the sets are infinite then things become much more interesting! In particular, we see opposite that the set of integers and the set of fractions are equivalent, whereas the set of integers (or fractions) and the set of real numbers are not equivalent—they have different *cardinalities*. As we see later, the *Continuum hypothesis* is the conjecture that every infinite subset of the real numbers is equivalent to either the set of integers (or fractions) or the set of real numbers.

Although Cantor's work on infinite sets caused great controversy at first, it was soon taken up by other mathematicians and was found to have important applications throughout the whole of mathematics.

Georg Cantor

Some Infinities are Larger Than Others

In his *Two New Sciences*, Galileo noted that *the set of positive integers* (1, 2, 3, ...) *is larger than the set of their squares* (1, 4, 9, ...), and yet *the two sets must have the same size* since we can match them up exactly: 1 ↔ 1, 2 ↔ 4, 3 ↔ 9, 4 ↔ 16, ...

We can also match up the positive integers with some larger sets, such as *all* the integers (positive, negative, and zero), by listing them in the order: 0, 1, –1, 2, –2, 3, –3, 4, ... ; notice that every integer occurs somewhere in this list. A set that can be matched up with the set of positive integers in this way is called *countable*, because we can list (or count) all its elements—so *the set of all integers is countable.*

Now look at all the fractions. Although this set seems much larger than the set of positive integers, Cantor made the unexpected discovery that we can list all the fractions in order—so *the set of all fractions is countable.* On the other hand, as he also proved, *the set of all real numbers is not countable.* It follows that the set of real numbers is strictly larger than the set of all fractions—and so *some infinite sets are bigger than others.* Cantor then took this idea further by proving that *there are infinitely many infinities, all of different sizes.*

THE SET OF ALL FRACTIONS IS COUNTABLE

We first list all the *positive* fractions, as shown: the first row lists the integers, the second row lists the "halves," and so on. We then "snake around" the diagonals of this array of numbers, deleting any numbers that we have seen before: this gives the list:

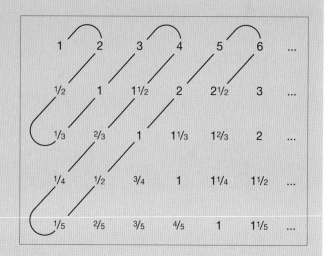

1, 2, ½, ⅓, 3, 4, 1½, ⅔, ¼, ⅕, 5, 6, 2½, ...

This list contains all the positive fractions.

To list *all* the fractions (positive, negative, and zero) in order, we then alternate + and –, as before. So the set of all fractions is countable.

THE SET OF ALL REAL NUMBERS IS NOT COUNTABLE

It is enough to prove that *the set of all numbers between 0 and 1 is not countable.*
To do so, we assume that this set is countable, and obtain a contradiction.
So, assuming that this set is countable, we can list its numbers (as decimals), as follows:

$$0 \cdot a_1\, a_2\, a_3\, a_4\, a_5 \ldots \,, \ 0 \cdot b_1\, b_2\, b_3\, b_4\, b_5 \ldots \,, \ 0 \cdot c_1\, c_2\, c_3\, c_4\, c_5 \ldots \,, \ 0 \cdot d_1\, d_2\, d_3\, d_4\, d_5 \ldots \,, \text{ etc.}$$

By our assumption, this list contains all the numbers between 0 and 1.

We obtain the required contradiction by constructing a new number between 0 and 1 that does not lie in this list. To do this, we choose numbers $X_1, X_2, X_3, X_4, \ldots$ from 1 to 9 such that:

$$X_1 \neq a_1, X_2 \neq b_2, X_3 \neq c_3, X_4 \neq d_4, \ldots \,, \text{ and consider the number } 0 \cdot X_1\, X_2\, X_3\, X_4 \ldots$$

Since $X_1 \neq a_1$, this new number differs from the first number in the list; since $X_2 \neq b_2$, it differs from the second number in the list; and so on.

Thus, this new number differs from every number in the list. This gives us the required contradiction. So the set of all numbers is not countable.

Felix Klein

Felix Klein (1849–1925) was a German mathematician who worked on geometry—particularly non-Euclidean geometry and the connection between geometry and group theory. At the University of Göttingen he developed the world's foremost mathematical center, where he was an influential educationalist and teacher. He was founder of the great mathematical Encyklopädie *and was editor of one of the leading mathematical journals of the time, the* Mathematische Annalen.

Klein was born in Düsseldorf and studied at Bonn, Göttingen, and Berlin. From 1872 to 1875 he was professor at Erlangen in Germany before moving to Munich, Leipzig, and finally to the University of Göttingen in 1886. As head of the mathematics department there, Klein proved to be a worthy successor to Gauss, Dirichlet, and Riemann. His school of mathematics was the most famous in the world and attracted many brilliant scholars.

Göttingen began admitting women in 1893, and one of Klein's doctoral students was Grace Chisholm (later, Grace Chisholm Young after her marriage), who gave an insight into the views held there:

Professor Klein's attitude is this, he will not countenance the admission of any woman who has not already done good work, and can bring proof of the same in the form of degrees or their equivalent … and further he will not take any further steps till he has assured himself by a personal interview of the solidity of her claims. Professor Klein's view is moderate. There are members of the Faculty here who are more eagerly in favor of the admission of women and others who disapprove altogether.

Klein dominated the institutional developments in German mathematics and was a prime mover for the organization of mathematics conferences. He also led an international team in the production of the multi-volume *Encyclopedia of Mathematical Science*, published between 1890 and 1920.

Right: *The Mathematics Club of Göttingen in 1902: at the table are David Hilbert, Felix Klein, Karl Schwarzschild, and Grace Chisholm.*

THE KLEIN BOTTLE

Klein's most familiar legacy is the surface known as a *Klein bottle.* It is constructed from a Möbius band by gluing its boundary edge to the boundary of a circular disc, and cannot exist in three dimensions without intersecting itself.

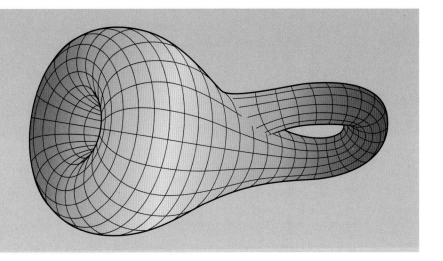

THE *ERLANGER PROGRAMM*

By 1870 the world of geometry had become very complicated. In addition to non-Euclidean geometry, there were Euclidean and spherical geometries, similarity, affine, and projective geometries, and many others besides. The remaining years of the century saw a variety of attempts to sort out the confusion and impose order on the subject.

The most famous of these was the *Erlanger Programm*, circulated in written form at Klein's inaugural lecture as professor at the University of Erlangen in 1872, when he was twenty-three. The lecture was aimed at a university-wide audience and was concerned with Klein's pedagogical views on mathematical education, the unity of all knowledge, and the importance of a complete and wide-ranging education.

In the *Erlanger Programm* Klein gave a new and remarkable definition of a "geometry" that helped to unify existing geometries and also provided a "road map" for future research. For him, a *geometry* was a set of points (such as the points in a plane) with transformations (such as rotations, reflections, and translations) defined upon it, where we are interested in those properties of the set that remain unchanged by the transformations:

> *Given a manifold [the set of points] and a group of transformations of the same; to investigate the configurations belonging to*

Felix Klein

the manifold with regard to such properties as are not altered by the transformations of the group.

For our example in the plane we obtain our familiar Euclidean geometry. Since our transformations do not alter size or shape, we are interested in such geometrical properties as the lengths of lines and the congruence between triangles.

If we now enlarge the group of transformations we can obtain other geometries. For example, if we also include *scalings* (that make figures larger or smaller), then we obtain a different geometry, sometimes called *similarity geometry*. Here the transformations preserve shape (but not size, in general), so fewer geometrical properties are preserved.

Continuing to enlarge the group of transformations produces a "hierarchy of geometries," all of which turn out to be contained in projective geometry. In particular, Euclidean and non-Euclidean geometries are both special cases of projective geometry, so any result in projective geometry is also true for them (and indeed for all other geometries). The task that Klein set himself, of unifying all geometries, had been achieved.

In 1923 Klein summarized his lifelong attitude to geometry:

> *I did not conceive of the word geometry one-sidedly as the subject of objects in space, but rather as a way of thinking that can be applied with profit in all domains of mathematics.*

THE MODERN AGE

In our final chapter we meet the mathematicians who have:

- *examined the limits of what we can prove and shown why some tasks are impossible to carry out;*
- *laid the foundations of our current scientific knowledge;*
- *carried out mathematical work of historical, social, and political impact, and thereby changed the world we live in;*
- *developed computers, both theoretical and practical, that enable us to simulate, model, and prove things that we could not do otherwise, while raising questions about our identity.*

PARADOXES AND PROBLEMS

In previous chapters we have seen a developing desire to place mathematics on a sounder foundation, with the story going from the underpinning notions of the calculus to arithmetic and the theory of sets. As twentieth-century mathematicians examined more carefully the nature of infinity and the problems connected with sets, they met a number of problems and paradoxes. One of the most famous of these was formulated by Bertrand Russell in 1902, and necessitated a much more thorough treatment of the very foundations of set theory and of the exact nature of deductive proof.

The Princeton Institute for Advanced Study, established in 1930: twenty-five Nobel Laureates and thirty-eight (out of fifty-two) Fields Medalists have been affiliated with it.

for his general theory of relativity, while algebra became an abstract and axiomatic subject, being particularly influenced by the work of Emmy Noether. Advances also continued to be made in number theory, with Hardy (and his co-workers Littlewood and Ramanujan) and Andrew Wiles making major contributions.

Meanwhile, new areas of the subject came into being, such as algebraic topology and the theory of "Hilbert spaces," while machine computation entered the mainstream of the subject, as spectacularly illustrated by Appel and Haken in their proof of the four-color theorem.

Another approach was taken by David Hilbert, whose attempt to make arithmetic secure was to make it *axiomatic*, an approach that he had already used with success when dealing with the foundations of geometry. Instead of defining all the basic terms, such as point or line, he gave a set of rules (or axioms) that they had to satisfy.

Although Hilbert's approach was influential, his objectives were eventually proved to be unattainable, as demonstrated in the 1930s by Kurt Gödel and Alan Turing, who obtained a number of amazing and unexpected results about the limits of what can be proved or decided.

ABSTRACTION AND GENERALIZATION

The nineteenth-century trend toward increasing generalization and abstraction continued to accelerate dramatically throughout the twentieth century. For example, Albert Einstein used the abstract formulations of geometry and calculus

SPREAD AND DEVELOPMENT

The twentieth century saw mathematics becoming a major profession throughout the world, with jobs in education and industry and numerous areas of specialization and application.

With mathematics developing at such a fast rate, many new journals have been created, and national and international conferences have become widespread. Most important among these meetings are the International Congresses of Mathematicians, hosted every four years by the International Mathematical Union, where the prestigious Fields Medals are awarded and many thousands of mathematicians gather to learn about the latest developments in their subject.

David Hilbert

On August 8, 1900, David Hilbert (1862–1943), one of the greatest mathematicians of the day, gave the most celebrated mathematical lecture of all time. For it was on this date, at the International Congress of Mathematicians in Paris, that he presented a list of unsolved problems for twentieth-century mathematicians to tackle. Trying to solve these problems helped to set the mathematical agenda for the next hundred years.

David Hilbert was born in Königsberg in Eastern Prussia and received his doctorate there in 1885. After teaching in Königsberg for a few years, he was invited by Felix Klein to join the faculty at Göttingen, where he spent the rest of his life.

His mathematical range was immense—from abstract number theory and invariant theory, via the calculus of variations and the study of analysis (and so-called Hilbert spaces), to potential theory and the kinetic theory of gases.

THE FOUNDATIONS OF GEOMETRY

Following Cantor's introduction of set theory and subsequent investigations by various mathematicians into the foundations of arithmetic, Hilbert became increasingly involved with the foundations of geometry.

Although Euclid's axiom system had worked well for two thousand years, it contained a number of unwarranted assumptions. Hilbert duly set about replacing it by alternative sets of axioms that were completely foolproof. His aim, in particular, was to find axiom systems that are:

- *consistent:* the axioms do not lead to contradictions;

- *independent:* no axiom can be deduced from the others;

- *complete:* any statement that we may formulate within the system can be proved to be either true or false.

In 1899 Hilbert produced his influential *Grundlagen der Geometrie* (Foundations of Geometry), in which he developed his axiom

David Hilbert

systems for Euclidean and projective geometry. Four years later he produced a second edition in which he also axiomatized non-Euclidean geometry.

Hilbert had a grand plan. He was convinced that the whole of classical mathematics could be similarly axiomatized, and with Paul Bernays he wrote a two-volume work with this purpose in mind. But as they progressed, they experienced unexpected difficulties with the details of their arguments, and it soon became apparent that Hilbert's plan was doomed to failure.

David Hilbert

THE HILBERT PROBLEMS

Who of us would not be glad to lift the veil behind which the future lies hidden: to cast a glance at the next advances of our science and at the secrets of its development during future centuries?

So asked David Hilbert in his famous address at the Paris Congress, at which he presented his list of twenty-three unsolved problems. We have already met one of these problems, the *Riemann hypothesis*, which remains unsolved to this day. Here we present a few more, some of which will be discussed later in this chapter.

Problem 1

Prove the Continuum hypothesis, that there is no set whose cardinality lies strictly between those of the integers and the real numbers.

We recall that Cantor proved that infinities can have different sizes, and that the set of real numbers is strictly larger than the set of integers (or fractions). This problem asks us to prove that no infinite set is larger than the set of integers but smaller than the set of real numbers.

Problem 2

Are the axioms of arithmetic consistent?

Hilbert based his treatment of the consistency of his geometrical axioms on the assumption that arithmetic (that is, our real number system) can be similarly axiomatized. This problem asks whether this latter assumption is valid, or whether there could be, "somewhere out there," a contradiction that we never expected.

Problem 3

Given two polyhedra with the same volume, can we always cut the first into finitely many pieces that can then be reassembled to give the second?

In 1833, János Bolyai proved that if two polygons have the same area, then the first can be cut into pieces that can be rearranged to give the second; the following example shows a triangle reassembled to give a square. This problem

asks whether a similar result holds in three dimensions.

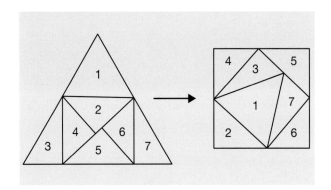

The answer is no. Within two years Max Dehn proved that a regular tetrahedron *cannot* be cut into pieces that can then be reassembled to give a cube with the same volume.

Problem 18

What is the most efficient way to stack spheres so that the amount of empty space between them is as small as possible?

This problem was considered by Harriot (c.1560–c.1621) and Kepler. Two ways to stack the spheres are cubic stacking and hexagonal stacking, but neither is the most efficient. It turns out that the way greengrocers stack oranges is the most efficient—the proportion of empty space is about 0.36, which is less than the 0.48 and 0.40 proportions of the other two. But to prove this rigorously was horrendous: in 1998 Thomas Hales gave a computer-aided proof that involved three gigabytes of computer power.

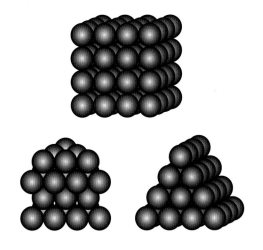

Cubic stacking, hexagonal stacking, and greengrocer's stacking

Henri Poincaré

Henri Poincaré (1854–1912) is viewed as one of the great geniuses of all time, being probably the last person to cover the entire range of mathematics. He virtually founded the theories of several complex variables and algebraic topology, and one of his conjectures in topology, known as the Poincaré conjecture, *was solved only in this century. He made outstanding contributions to differential equations and non-Euclidean geometry, and also worked on electricity, magnetism, quantum theory, hydrodynamics, elasticity, the special theory of relativity, and the philosophy of science. As an active popularizer of his subject, he wrote popular works for non-mathematicians, stressing the importance of mathematics and science and discussing the psychology of mathematical discovery.*

Poincaré was born in Nancy, Northern France, and displayed great ability and interest in mathematics from a young age. He came from a distinguished family, and his cousin, Raymond Poincaré, became President of the French Republic during World War I. He attended the École Polytechnique in 1873, and after graduating went to the École des Mines for further study. In 1879 he obtained a post at the University of Caen, moving two years later to the University of Paris, where he remained until his death at the age of fifty-eight.

Below: *Henri Poincaré*

Analysis Situs

Although topology had its origins in the problem of the bridges of Königsberg and the theory of polyhedra, it was Poincaré and his successors who transformed it into a rich and powerful new way of looking at geometrical objects. Poincaré's work *Analysis Situs* (Analysis of Position), published in 1895, used algebraic methods to distinguish between surfaces and was an early systematic account of what we now call *algebraic topology*.

the coordinates of each point as a series in a variable that is some known function of time and for all of whose values the series converges uniformly.

Newton had solved this problem for two bodies, and Poincaré responded to the king's challenge by attacking a special case of the problem when there are only three bodies (the *restricted three-body problem*), hoping that he would eventually be able to generalize his results to the general three-body problem, and then to more than three bodies.

By considering approximations to the orbits, he was able to make considerable progress, developing valuable new techniques in analysis along the way. Although he could not solve the three-body problem in its entirety, he developed so much new mathematics in his attempts that he was awarded the prize.

However, while his paper was being prepared for publication, one of the editors queried it, unable to follow Poincaré's arguments. Poincaré realized that he had made a mistake: contrary to what he formerly thought, even a small change in the initial conditions can produce vastly different orbits. This meant that his approximations did not give him the results he had expected. But this led to something even more important. The orbits that Poincaré discovered were what we now call chaotic: he had stumbled on the mathematics at the basis of modern-day *chaos theory*, where even with deterministic laws the resulting motion may be irregular and unpredictable.

THE POINCARÉ DISC

One difficulty caused by the non-Euclidean geometry of Bolyai and Lobachevsky was that it was hard to visualize. A number of pictorial representations were suggested, the most successful being the "disc model," discovered by Poincaré in 1880.

Consider the following picture of a disc (the inside of a circle). We consider a geometry in which the *points* are those lying inside the bounding circle, and the *lines* are either diameters that pass through the center of the disc or circular arcs that meet the bounding circle at right angles.

As we can see:

- some pairs of *lines* (diameters or circular arcs) do not meet;
- some pairs of *lines* meet at internal *points;*
- some pairs of *lines* meet on the bounding circle: such *lines* are said to be *parallel.*

With these definitions of *point* and *line*, Euclid's first four axioms are satisfied, but not the fifth, so we do indeed have a non-Euclidean geometry. In this geometry many Euclidean concepts (such as size and shape) are no longer appropriate; for example, all the colored and white triangles in the picture turn out to be congruent to each other! The Dutch artist Maurits Escher based some of his woodcuts (such as *Circle Limit IV*) on this picture of a non-Euclidean geometry.

Russell and Gödel

Bertrand Russell (1872–1970) and Kurt Gödel (1906–78) were the most important logicians of the twentieth century. In the early years of the century the foundations of mathematics were in turmoil. Russell's celebrated paradox caused major difficulties which took time to resolve. Meanwhile, as Hilbert and others were continuing with their ambitious program of sorting out the foundations of arithmetic, Gödel upset the apple-cart with his startling results on the completeness and consistency of axiom systems.

Bertrand Russell was one of the outstanding figures of the twentieth century. Born of a noble family, he was orphaned as a young child and brought up by his grandmother, before going to Trinity College, Cambridge, to study both mathematics and the moral sciences. A vigorous peace campaigner, he was twice imprisoned for his anti-war activities. In 1950 he was awarded the Nobel Prize for Literature.

Kurt Gödel was born in Vienna. He suffered from rheumatic fever at the age of six, and from then on was constantly obsessed with his health. After graduating from the University of Vienna in mathematics, he wrote his doctoral thesis there on mathematical logic and joined the faculty. In 1940 he emigrated to the USA, where he spent the rest of his distinguished career at the Princeton Institute for Advanced Study, receiving many awards and becoming a close friend of Albert Einstein. He suffered from paranoia and, convinced that he was being poisoned, refused to eat and died of malnutrition.

Kurt Gödel receives an award from Albert Einstein.

RUSSELL'S PARADOX

The German logician Gottlob Frege was on the point of sending a book on axiomatics to his publishers when he received a letter from Bertrand Russell, effectively saying:

> *Dear Gottlob, Consider the set of all sets that are not members of themselves. Bertrand.*

This paradox demolished much of his book, and mathematical logic was changed for ever.

A simpler version of Russell's paradox concerns a village barber who shaves all those who do not shave themselves, but does not shave those who do shave themselves. The question arises: *Who shaves the barber?*

- If the barber shaves himself, we obtain a contradiction since he does not shave those who shave themselves.

- But if the barber does not shave himself, we obtain a contradiction since he shaves all those who don't shave themselves.

Thus, this problem can have no answer.

Russell's version of his paradox had asked: *let S be the set of all*

Left: *Bertrand Russell*

Kurt Gödel and Hilbert's Problems

In 1931 Gödel produced a paper that changed mathematics for ever. His first "bombshell," the *Incompleteness theorem*, was to prove that:

In any axiomatic system that includes the integers, there are true results that cannot be proved, and there are "undecidable" results that cannot be proved either true or false.

Hilbert's Problem 1
We saw earlier that Hilbert asked for a proof of the *Continuum hypothesis*, that no set is larger than the set of integers but smaller than the set of real numbers. Using his Incompleteness theorem, Gödel proved that, if we use Zermelo–Fraenkel set theory, then the *Continuum hypothesis cannot be disproved*. But in 1963 the American mathematician Paul Cohen stunned the mathematical world (thereby winning a Fields Medal) by proving that, under the same conditions, the *Continuum hypothesis cannot be proved*. Combining these results, we deduce that:

The Continuum hypothesis cannot be proved either true or false—it is "undecidable."

Hilbert's Problem 2
We recall that this asked us to prove that the axioms of arithmetic are consistent, so that contradictions cannot occur—but then Gödel produced a second bombshell by proving that:

The consistency of any theory that includes the integers cannot be proved within the theory itself— in other words, we cannot prove that contradictions can never occur.

One might have thought that these results would have finished off the subject for good—but most mathematicians chose to ignore them and carried on regardless.

---

sets that are not members of themselves. Is S a member of itself? Whether the answer is *yes* or *no*, we obtain contradictions similar to those above.

The appearance of Russell's paradox led philosophers and mathematicians to study set theory more carefully, and a number of versions emerged that could deal with such paradoxes more or less satisfactorily. Of these, the most successful and universally accepted was the *Zermelo–Fraenkel set theory*, due originally to Ernst Zermelo of Göttingen, and revised by Adolf Fraenkel of Marburg.

PRINCIPIA MATHEMATICA

Between 1910 and 1913 Bertrand Russell and his Cambridge colleague Alfred North Whitehead wrote a pioneering three-volume work entitled *Principia Mathematica*. Based partly

on ideas of Cantor and Frege, it was designed to deduce the whole of mathematics from a small number of basic principles. Below is their proof of the proposition "1 + 1 = 2."

Einstein and Minkowski

Albert Einstein (1879–1955), an iconic figure of the twentieth century, was the greatest mathematical physicist since Isaac Newton. He revolutionized physics with his theories of special and general relativity. These drew on mathematical ideas, not previously used in physics, some of which had been developed by Riemann and by Hermann Minkowski (1864–1909).

Einstein was born in Ulm, Southern Germany, and moved to Munich in 1880. He was slow in learning to speak and showed little promise in his early schooling. He was admitted to Zürich polytechnic at his second attempt in 1896 to a course for mathematics and science teachers and graduated in 1900. Although one of his lecturers was Minkowski, he gained little from the formal teaching and preferred to read independently and think deeply about the fundamental ideas and assumptions of physics. After graduation he supported himself by part-time teaching until he obtained a position in the Swiss Patent Office in Bern.

In 1905 Einstein submitted his paper on special relativity to the University of Bern in support of his application for a doctorate, and it was rejected! However, recognition of his work soon arrived as it became more widely known. He then held positions at the Universities of Zürich, Prague, and Berlin, and announced his general theory of relativity in 1915. He was awarded the Nobel Prize in 1921 for his work on quantum theory, rather than relativity. In 1933 he went to the United States and from then on was based at the Institute for Advanced Study in Princeton.

Left: *Albert Einstein— a plaque in Ulm*

EINSTEIN'S *ANNUS MIRABILIS*

In 1905, his "year of wonders," Albert Einstein published four papers of real ground-breaking importance. First he published the work that introduced *quanta of energy*—that light can be absorbed or emitted only in discrete amounts, a central idea of quantum theory. After this he produced a paper on Brownian motion, which explained the movement of small particles suspended in a stationary liquid.

Einstein's third paper, concerning the electrodynamics of moving bodies, introduced a new theory linking time, distance, mass, and energy. It was consistent with electromagnetism, but omitted the force of gravity. This became known as the *special theory of relativity* and assumed that c, the speed of light, is constant, irrespective of where you are or how you move.

On November 21, 1905 he published *Does the Inertia of a Body Depend Upon Its Energy Content?* This paper contains one of the most famous equations of all, $E = mc^2$, asserting the equivalence of mass and energy.

MINKOWSKI AND SPECIAL RELATIVITY

Minkowski was born of German parents in Lithuania. In 1902 he moved to the University of Göttingen, where he became a colleague of Hilbert. He developed a new view of space and time and laid the mathematical foundations of the theory of relativity. Minkowski described his approach as follows:

Henceforth space by itself, and time by itself, are doomed to fade away into mere shadows, and only a kind of union of the two will preserve an independent reality.

The kind of union that Minkowski mentions is now known as space-time and is a four-dimensional non-Euclidean geometry that incorporates the three dimensions of space with the one of time. It comes with a way of measuring the distance between two different points of space-time. Space and time are now no longer separate, as Newton had thought, but are intermixed. A reviewer said of his work that:

Hermann Minkowski

purely mathematical considerations, including harmony and elegance of ideas, should dominate in embracing new physical facts. Mathematics, so to speak, was to be master and physical theory could be made to bow to the master.

Below is a simplified diagram of space-time with only one space dimension going horizontally and with time going vertically. In Euclidean geometry the distance of each point (x, t) to the origin is $\sqrt{(x^2 + t^2)}$, but the requirements of relativity replace this in space-time with the distance $\sqrt{(x^2 - c^2t^2)}$. The minus sign implies that events in space-time, such as the one labeled "here and now," are associated with two cones. With just one space dimension, these cones are now triangles, with one representing the future of the "here and now" and the other its past.

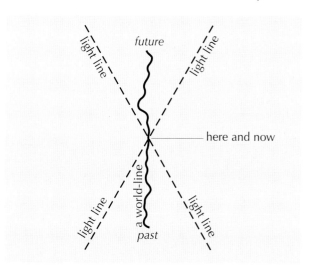

GENERAL RELATIVITY

Einstein initially thought little of Minkowski's approach to space-time, but later found it invaluable, indeed essential, when he was trying to extend his theory to include gravity. His *general theory of gravity*, building also on Riemann's geometrical ideas, produced space-time that was curved as a result of the presence of mass and energy. The curvature increased near to massive bodies, and it was the curvature of space-time that controlled the motion of bodies.

The theory predicted that light rays would be bent by the curvature of space-time produced by the sun, an effect that was observed during the 1919 solar eclipse of the sun.

Emmy Noether

Emmy Noether (1882–1935) was one of the most distinguished mathematicians of the twentieth century, contributing to invariant theory, the theory of relativity, and, especially, algebra. But being a woman and Jewish, she found herself subjected to great prejudice at several stages of her career.

Emmy Noether was born in Erlangen in Germany, where her father, the algebraist Max Noether, was professor of mathematics. At school she excelled in languages and trained to be a language teacher. But in 1900 she decided to change direction and studied mathematics at the University of Erlangen, where women were allowed to attend classes unofficially with

Emmy Noether

the lecturers' permission. She passed her final university examinations in 1903.

During the following winter she attended the University of Göttingen, where she went to lectures by Hilbert, Klein, and Minkowski, but returned to Erlangen where women were now accepted as students. She became officially registered there, and three years later was awarded a doctorate for a thesis in invariant theory.

At this stage she wished to return to Göttingen, but the regulations did not allow women to hold academic positions there. So she remained in Erlangen, helping her ailing father with his teaching commitments, while continuing with her academic research and publishing several papers. Her academic reputation began to spread and she was invited to give a number of prestigious lectures.

MATHEMATICAL PHYSICS IN GÖTTINGEN

In 1915, the year of Albert Einstein's general theory of relativity, Hilbert and Klein invited Emmy Noether back to Göttingen. Hilbert was also working on general relativity, and Noether was welcomed because of her deep knowledge of invariant theory.

Before long, she proved *Noether's theorem*, a cornerstone of general relativity and particle physics, which relates any conservation law in physics to invariance or symmetry properties. On learning of her result, Einstein wrote to Hilbert:

I'm impressed that such things can be understood in such a general way. The old guard at Göttingen should take some lessons from Miss Noether! She seems to know her stuff.

Right: *Bryn Mawr College*

Meanwhile, Hilbert and Klein were fighting the authorities to permit her to lecture in the University. Although Hilbert enabled her to do so by advertising her lectures under his own name, others, such as the philosophical faculty, were bitterly opposed, exclaiming:

What will our soldiers think when they return to the university and find that they are required to learn at the feet of a woman?

Hilbert angrily replied that the candidate's sex was of no importance, concluding with his memorable riposte:

We are a university, not a bath-house.

The battle was finally won in 1919.

ALGEBRA

Noether continued to write papers on invariant theory and relativity until 1920, when she had a change of direction and became interested in algebra—and in particular, the study of commutative rings. It is for her work in this area that she is best remembered.

Earlier we met the idea of a *group*, an algebraic object that consists of a set of elements and a single way of combining them in pairs so as to satisfy certain specified rules. Another algebraic object of interest is a *ring*, which consists of a set of elements and *two* ways of combining them in pairs so as to satisfy certain specified rules. Examples of rings include:

- adding and multiplying integers to give other integers;

- adding and multiplying complex numbers to give other complex numbers;

- adding and multiplying polynomials to give other polynomials;

- adding and multiplying matrices (rectangular arrays of numbers) to give other matrices.

If, moreover, multiplication is commutative—that is, $a \times b = b \times a$, for all elements a and b in the set—then we have a *commutative ring*. The first three of the above rings are commutative, but not the last one.

In 1921 Emmy Noether wrote a classic paper, *Idealtheorie in Ringbereichen* (Theory of Ideals in Ring Domains), in which she investigated the internal structure of commutative rings in terms of certain subsets called ideals. In particular, she studied rings in which a particular property of these ideals holds, and such rings are now known as *Noetherian rings*. Her researches in algebra continued throughout the 1920s and were rewarded with invitations to speak at the International Congresses of Mathematicians in Bologna in 1928 and Zürich in 1932.

LEAVING GERMANY

In 1933, with the rise of Adolf Hitler, the Nazi party withdrew the right of Jews to teach at the University, and Emmy was forced to leave Germany and seek employment elsewhere.

Eventually she was given a position at Bryn Mawr, a women's college near Philadelphia in the United States, and was also invited to lecture at the Institute for Advanced Study in Princeton. She was blissfully happy at Bryn Mawr, with congenial colleagues, but less than two years after arriving there she developed a large ovarian cyst and died.

John von Neumann

The enormous range of interests of John von Neumann (1903–57) is remarkable. He worked on the foundations of set theory and quantum mechanics, developed the algebra of operators on a Hilbert space, and founded the subject of game theory. His work on mathematical physics, particularly in turbulence, detonation waves, and shocks in fluids, was very influential. He advanced the theory of cellular automata, and with his introduction of the stored program concept is often called "the Father of Modern Computing."

Von Neumann was born in Budapest where, in 1926, he received his doctorate with a thesis on set theory. By his mid-twenties, he had an international reputation in the academic community. He lectured at Berlin and Hamburg until 1930, and for part of that time also studied with Hilbert at Göttingen. He then taught for three years at Princeton University until he was appointed as one of the founding professors at the newly created Princeton Institute for Advanced Study, a position he held for the rest of his life.

During and after World War II, von Neumann was an adviser to the American military on weapons development, in particular on atomic weapons and logistics. From 1943 to 1955 he was a consultant to the Los Alamos Scientific Laboratory. It has been suggested that the cancer that caused his death may have arisen from his being a witness at atomic bomb testings.

politics, and military strategy. His 1944 book with his Princeton colleague, Oskar Morgenstern, revolutionized the field of economics.

A *zero-sum game* between two players is one in which the gain to the winning player exactly equals the loss to the loser, so the total payoff to both players sums to zero. In 1928 von Neumann published his *minimax theorem* which proves, for a zero-sum two-person game, that both participants have strategies (or methods of playing) that minimize their maximum loss. As he remarked:

> *As far as I can see, there could be no theory of games … without that theorem … I thought there was nothing worth publishing until the "Minimax Theorem" was proved.*

His theory was later expanded to cover more general situations.

Oskar Morgenstern

GAME THEORY

Von Neumann's work on games is characteristic of a lifelong approach of using mathematics in practical situations. The consequences of his work go far beyond its applications to games of chance, such as poker, and have been important in psychology, sociology,

COMPUTING

After the war von Neumann led a team at Princeton in the development of a computer. They decided that it should have four main components:

- An arithmetic/logic unit, now called the central processing unit (CPU), which is where the basic elementary operations are performed: this was analogous to Babbage's mill.

- A memory (analogous to Babbage's store) that stored the numbers on which the calculations

were to be performed and also the instructions for performing the calculations. Since these instructions could be coded as numbers, the machine needed to be able to distinguish between numbers and coded instructions.

- A control unit that decoded and executed the instructions fetched from the memory.

- Input/output devices to allow data and instructions to be entered into the computer and the results of the calculations displayed. Von Neumann was particularly interested in output devices that could display results graphically.

Because it used electronic technology, numbers in the machine were represented in binary form, so that any device holding a digit needed to have only two states.

The machine was completed in 1952. It had 3,600 vacuum tubes and was the first stored

Above: *John von Neumann (right) and Robert Oppenheimer with the EDVAC computer*

program computer, unlike previous computers that were programed by altering their circuitry. Although it had its drawbacks, von Neumann's design model was very influential in the subsequent development of computers.

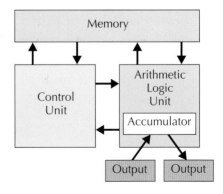

Von Neumann design architecture

Alan Turing

Alan Turing (1912–54) was a mathematician, logician, philosopher, codebreaker, and a founder of computer science. He is remembered for the Turing machine *which formalized the ideas of algorithm and computation, and the* Turing test *in artificial or machine intelligence. His codebreaking activities during World War II attacked the operation of the German cipher machines, with a subtle analysis of their logical structure.*

Alan Turing was born in London and entered King's College, Cambridge, in 1931, being elected to a fellowship there after graduating. In 1936 he went to Princeton University to pursue doctoral studies, but returned to Cambridge in 1938.

When war was declared, Turing moved to the Government Code and Cypher School at Bletchley Park. At the end of the war, he transferred to the National Physical Laboratory in London to work on the design of an electronic computer, the Automatic Computing Engine (ACE). His final university position was as Deputy Director of the Manchester Computing Laboratory.

Turing continued to be consulted by GCHQ, the successor to Bletchley Park, but lost his security clearance when he was brought to trial for homosexual activities in 1952. He came under intense scrutiny by the intelligence services, who regarded him as a security risk. He died of cyanide poisoning, a half-eaten apple beside his bed, and the inquest brought in a verdict of suicide.

Alan Turing

TURING MACHINE

Turing was intrigued by Hilbert's decision problem, a problem in mathematical logic:

> *Given a mathematical proposition, can one find an algorithm to decide whether the proposition is true or false?*

To tackle this, Turing needed a workable definition of an algorithm, and he identified this with the output of an abstract machine, later called a *Turing machine*, which consisted of an infinite tape and a component that could be in any one of a finite number of states. These states could change, depending on the current symbol that was read from the tape.

He then went a step further and envisaged a *universal Turing machine* that could emulate all other Turing machines—an analogy is the modern computer which can do different tasks if its programing is altered appropriately. In 1936 Turing answered the question in the negative: there are mathematical propositions

Growth and Form in Biology

Turing had a lifelong interest in the development of pattern and form in living organisms. Toward the end of his life he applied various mathematical techniques to the subject. He particularly wanted to explain the appearance of Fibonacci numbers in plants—for example, in the spiral patterns in sunflower heads.

He first looked at how biological systems that are symmetrical at the start can lose that symmetry, and wondered how this could be caused by the dynamics of the way that the chemicals diffuse and react. Using a computer, he carried out pioneering work in modeling these chemical reactions, and published his results in his 1952 paper, *The Chemical Basis of Morphogenesis.*

that are *undecidable*—no algorithm can decide whether they are true or false. The idea of a Turing machine became the foundation of the theory of computation.

BLETCHLEY PARK

Bletchley Park, near Milton Keynes in Buckinghamshire, England, was the home of the British codebreaking efforts in World War II. There, Turing and his colleagues attacked the codes generated by the German electromechanical rotor-coding machines *Enigma* and *Lorenz*.

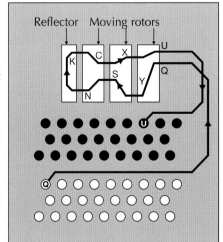

In the example illustrated below left, when a key is pressed a current flows through the three rotors, is reflected, and then flows back through the rotors to light up a lamp to give the code for the pressed key. Then, crucially, one of the rotors rotates, creating a new pathway for the signals. When the first rotor has made a complete rotation, as a result of key presses, the middle rotor begins to move, and when it has made a complete rotation, the last rotor starts to move.

A logical feature of this machine is that, in any given state of the rotors, the coding is symmetrical. For example, if letter Q is coded as letter U, then U would be coded as Q; in particular, it can never code a letter into itself. Turing used such an analysis of the logical structure of the machine to allow the successful decoding of messages.

The official historian of British Intelligence in World War II has said that the intelligence provided by Bletchley Park shortened the war "by not less than two years and probably by four years."

THE TURING TEST

In his 1950 paper, *Computing Machinery and Intelligence*, published in the journal *Mind*, Turing begins:

I propose to consider the question, "Can machines think?"

He refined this question by having a machine, a woman, and an interrogator, with the interrogator in a separate room from the other two subjects. The object of the game, known as the *Turing test,* is for the interrogator to determine which of the two subjects is the machine and which is the woman. They can communicate with the interrogator, but only in a manner that gives no clue to their identities.

In his previous work with Turing machines, he had concentrated on what machines cannot do. Now his focus was on what machines can do, and in particular whether the behavior of the brain can be replicated by a computer.

The Turing test remains an important tool in philosophy and artificial intelligence to this day.

Benoît Mandelbrot

An exciting area of mathematics that emerged in the twentieth century, although it can trace its origins back to Bolzano and Poincaré, is that of fractal geometry. This topic was espoused and greatly developed by Benoît Mandelbrot (1924–2010), and is closely associated with the fashionable area of chaos theory.

Mandelbrot was born in Poland and spent most of his working life at the computer firm IBM in the United States. He joined Yale University at the age of seventy-five and retired in 2005.

How long is the coastline of an island? If you look at Britain, for example, from far above the earth, or if you try to measure it with a ruler, you can estimate the length of the coastline. But as you measure more accurately, or get closer to the earth, you become aware of more and more inlets and bays, and the length increases accordingly. The closer you get, the longer the coastline seems to become. In fact, the coastline of Britain has infinite length, even though it encloses a finite area.

Benoît Mandelbrot

VON KOCH'S SNOWFLAKE CURVE

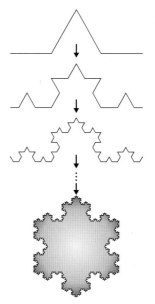

A similar situation occurs with the *snowflake curve*, described in 1906 by the Swedish mathematician Helge von Koch. To construct it, take an equilateral triangle, and then replace the middle third of each side (which we can think of as the base of a smaller equilateral triangle) by the other two sides of the triangle, giving a "peak" on each side of the original triangle.

Now repeat this process with each of the lines in the resulting picture. Carrying on this process for ever gives the snowflake curve.

Like the coastline of Britain, the snowflake has infinite length, yet encloses a finite area. It is also *self-similar*—parts of it have the same shape (though smaller) when you look at it in closer detail. This self-similarity is a standard feature of fractal patterns, a topic of great interest in the twentieth century.

THE MANDELBROT SET

A new way of obtaining fractal patterns was described by Benoît Mandelbrot. Consider the transformation $z \rightarrow z^2 + c$, where c is a fixed complex number. For each initial value, square it and add c to give a new number, and continually repeat the process. For example, when $c = 0$ and $z \rightarrow z^2$:

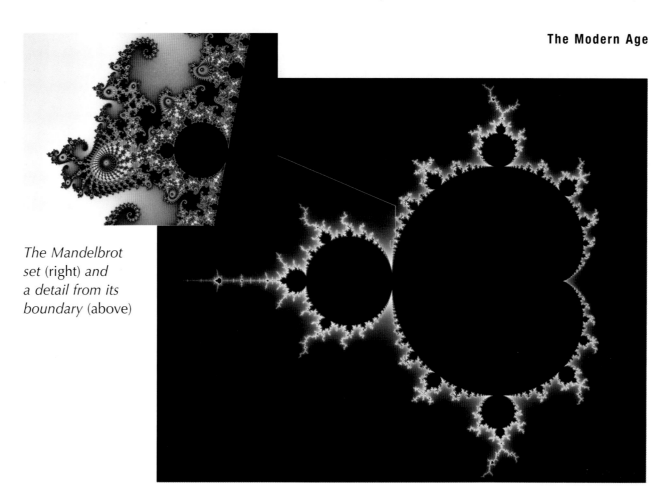

The Mandelbrot set (right) *and a detail from its boundary* (above)

- the initial value 2 gives 4, 16, 256, ... , going off to infinity;

- the initial value ½ gives ¼, ¹/₁₆, ¹/₂₅₆, ... , which tends to 0.

Here, all points inside the circle with center 0 and radius 1 stay inside the circle, all points on the circle stay on the circle, and all points outside the circle go to infinity.

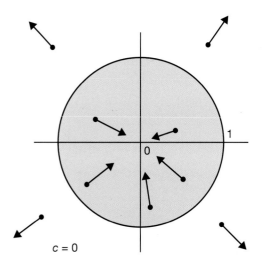

$c = 0$

We call this boundary circle the *Julia set for c =* 0 (after the French mathematician Gaston Julia), and its inside is the keep set (because we keep its points in sight).

Different values of c give a wide range of different boundary curves (Julia sets): for example, $c = 0.25$ gives us a "cauliflower" shape, while $c = -0.123 + 0.745i$ gives us a shape somewhat like a rabbit. The Julia sets for some values of c are in one piece, while others are in several pieces.

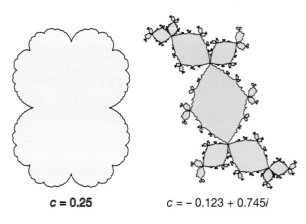

$c = 0.25$ $c = -0.123 + 0.745i$

Two Julia sets

Mandelbrot drew a picture of all the complex numbers c for which the Julia set is in one piece, obtaining a fascinating picture now called the *Mandelbrot set.* This set arises in the study of chaos theory, where it shows how sensitive the behavior of the transformation can be on the choice of the number c. It has given rise to a whole range of beautiful designs under the heading of *fractal art.*

Andrew Wiles

It is not given to everyone to achieve their childhood dream, but this happened for Sir Andrew Wiles (b.1953), who encountered Fermat's last theorem as a schoolboy, worked on it single-mindedly for many years, and eventually proved it after a lengthy and difficult struggle and a magical moment.

Wiles recalls when he first came across Fermat's last theorem:

> *One day I happened to be looking in my public library and I found a book on maths—it told a bit about the history of this problem and I, a ten-year-old, could understand it. From that moment I tried to solve it myself—it was such a challenge, such a beautiful problem— this problem was Fermat's last theorem.*

Wiles studied at Oxford University and then took his doctorate at Cambridge. He spent some time at Harvard University and in Germany before taking up an appointment at the Institute for Advanced Study in Princeton, where he spent almost twenty years. He has now returned to Oxford University as a Royal Society Research Professor.

FERMAT'S LAST THEOREM

Earlier, we saw that Fermat proved that the equation $x^4 + y^4 = z^4$ has no positive integer solutions x, y, and z, and that Euler proved a similar result for the equation $x^3 + y^3 = z^3$. But "Fermat's last theorem," which asserts that:

> *For any integer n (> 2), there are no positive integers x, y, and z for which $x^n + y^n = z^n$,*

remained unproved for all larger values of n.

In order to prove Fermat's last theorem in general, it is enough to prove it when n is a prime number—for example, we can reduce the case $n = 20$ to the case $n = 5$ by writing:

$$x^{20} + y^{20} = z^{20} \quad \text{as} \quad X^5 + Y^5 = Z^5$$

where $X = x^4$, $Y = y^4$ and $Z = z^4$

In the nineteenth century, proofs were found for $n = 5$ and $n = 7$, and the German number-theorist Ernst Kummer proved it also for a large class of primes called "regular primes." Much later, building on his work, and making extensive use of modern computers, the list was extended to all primes below 4,000,000.

THE BREAKTHROUGH

Two ideas that were central to Wiles's eventual proof are those of an "elliptic curve" and a "modular form." An *elliptic curve* is essentially a curve whose equation is of the form:

$$y^2 = x^3 + rx^2 + sx + t$$

for some integers r, s, and t. A *modular form* may be thought of, in general terms, as a way of generalizing the Möbius transformation:

$$f(z) = (az + b) / (cz + d)$$

Yutaka Taniyama and Goro Shimura conjectured that *Every elliptic curve is associated with a*

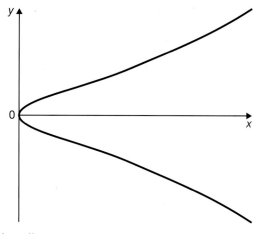

The elliptic curve $y^2 = x^3 + x$

modular form, and it was quickly realized that a proof of this conjecture (or at least a special case of it) would imply the truth of Fermat's last theorem.

Around 1984 major progress was made when Gerhard Frey of Saarbrücken spotted that if Fermat's theorem were false, so that the equation $a^p + b^p = c^p$ held for some positive integers a, b, and c and prime number p, then the elliptic curve:

$$y^2 = x^3 + (b^p - a^p)\, x^2 - a^p b^p\, x$$

would have such bizarre properties that it could not be modular, thereby contradicting the Taniyama–Shimura conjecture.

THE PROOF

At this stage, Andrew Wiles entered the fray. Excited by Frey's observations, he set himself the task of proving the special case of the Taniyama–Shimura conjecture that implied the truth of Fermat's last theorem. For seven years he hid himself away from other distractions while he concentrated on chipping away at the problem:

You cannot focus yourself for years unless you have this kind of undivided concentration which too many spectators would destroy.

By 1993 he had convinced himself that he had completed the proof, and he presented it, to world-wide enthusiasm and acclaim, at a major conference at Cambridge University.

Above: *Andrew Wiles lectures on elliptic curves.*

But during the detailed checking of the proof by the great and the good, a serious gap was discovered. For over a year, Wiles and his former doctoral student, Richard Taylor, struggled to close the gap. Wiles was about to give up when:

Suddenly, unexpectedly, I had this incredible revelation. It was the most important moment of my working life.

Nothing I ever do again … it was so indescribably beautiful, it was so simple and so elegant, and I just stared in disbelief for twenty minutes, then during the day I walked around the department. I'd keep coming back to my desk to see it was still there—it was still there.

The proof was indeed complete, and Andrew Wiles was able to look back with pride and pleasure on his monumental achievement:

There is no other problem that will mean the same to me. I had this very rare privilege of being able to pursue in my adult life what had been my childhood dream. I know it's a rare privilege, but I know if one can do this, it's more rewarding than anything one can imagine.

Andrew Wiles was made a Knight Commander of the Order of the British Empire by Queen Elizabeth in 2000.

Grigori Perelman

In August 2000, a century after Hilbert had introduced his twenty-three problems in Paris, seven "millennium problems" were announced, in order to celebrate mathematics in the new millennium. These "Himalayas of mathematics," each carrying a reward of one million dollars for its solution, were considered by the mathematical community to be the most difficult and important in the subject. One of these is the Riemann hypothesis, *which remains unsolved. Another was the* Poincaré conjecture, *posed by Poincaré in 1904, which was recently solved by the Russian mathematician Grigori Perelman (b. 1966).*

Topology, sometimes referred to as "bendy geometry," is the branch of geometry in which two shapes are regarded as the same whenever we can bend, or deform, either into the other. For example, the sphere and the torus are not the same, since we cannot deform either into the other, whereas we can deform a sphere into a cube, or a torus into a teacup. Indeed, a topologist has been described as someone who cannot tell the difference between a bagel and a teacup!

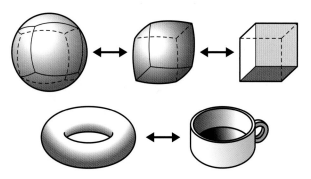

Another way of explaining why the sphere and the torus are not the same is to lay a loop of thread on the surface and try to shrink it to a point. With the sphere you can place the loop anywhere and it will always shrink to a point. On the torus you sometimes can—but not always, because the hole might get in the way.

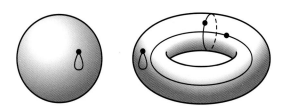

We now restrict our attention to the surfaces of spheres, but vary the dimension:

- We consider a circle to be one-dimensional, even though it lives in two-dimensional space, because it is a "bent-around line": the equation of such a "one-dimensional sphere" is $x^2 + y^2 = r^2$, where r is the radius.

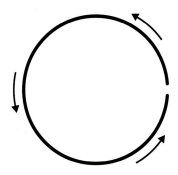

- If we now fill in two circles, bend them, and glue corresponding points together, we get a sphere (see below). We consider this sphere to be two-dimensional, even though it lives in three-dimensional space—think of standing on the surface of the earth and viewing the two-dimensional world around you: the equation of such a "two-dimensional sphere" is $x^2 + y^2 + z^2 = r^2$.

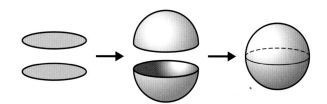

- We can continue in this way. To get a three-dimensional sphere, we take two solid spheres and glue corresponding points together: although this cannot be done, or visualized, in our three-dimensional world, it can still be studied mathematically, giving us an object that lives in four-dimensional space: the equation of such a "three-dimensional sphere" is $x^2 + y^2 + z^2 + w^2 = r^2$.

- In the same way, we can consider four-dimensional, five-dimensional, and even higher-dimensional, spheres.

THE POINCARÉ CONJECTURE

In two dimensions, it can be proved that:

The surface of a sphere (or any surface that can be deformed into a sphere) is the only surface with the loop-shrinking property.

The torus does not have this property, as we saw, and nor does any other type of surface. But what happens in higher dimensions?

Is the surface of a higher-dimensional sphere the only surface with the loop-shrinking property?

Poincaré conjectured that the answer to the last question is yes, and this became known as the *Poincaré conjecture*. For the two-dimensional sphere the answer is *yes*, as we have seen, and in the 1960s the American mathematician Stephen Smale proved that the answer is also *yes* for surfaces of dimension 5 or higher. Then, in 1982, another American mathematician, Michael Freedman, proved it for surfaces of dimension 4.

But what about surfaces of dimension 3? This seemed to be the hardest case. No one could prove it, and in this form it became one of the seven millennium problems.

PERELMAN'S SOLUTION

Perelman was a mathematical prodigy. In his student days he participated in the USSR team in the International Mathematical Olympiad, where he achieved a perfect score.

In 2002 and 2003 he published several papers in which he succeeded in proving the *Poincaré conjecture*. His solution was very difficult to understand, even for specialists. To analyze the surfaces concerned, he essentially looked at the various ways in which a liquid can flow over them, and studied the dynamics of these so-called Ricci flows; these are somewhat like the flow of heat through a solid object.

His papers caused a sensation throughout the mathematical world. But Perelman shuns publicity, believing passionately that mathematics should be studied for its own sake alone and not for any financial reward. Smale and Freedman both received Fields Medals for their contributions to the solution of the Poincaré conjecture, but when Perelman was offered one at the International Congress of Mathematicians in 2006, he turned it down. Four years later he turned down the million-dollar prize offered to him for solving one of the millennium problems. He is reported to have said during an interview:

I'm not a hero of mathematics. I'm not even that successful; that is why I don't want to have everybody looking at me.

Grigori Perelman

Glossary

algorithm A rule for carrying out a calculation.

analytic geometry Geometry using coordinates.

axiom A basic law that is self-evident and requires no proof.

base The basis of a counting system; the base number is that to which numbers are counted before shifting the place value (to tens, hundreds, etc).

binary Counting system that has only two digits, 1 and 0 (base 2).

binomial coefficients The sequence of coefficients used with variables when a binomial expression is expanded.

calculus The branch of mathematics concerned with calculating the sum of infinitesimal quantities to approximate the area under a curve or the rate of change of a curve.

chord A straight line joining the ends of an arc (a portion of the circumference of a circle).

coefficient A constant or number by which a variable is multiplied in an algebraic expression.

conics The family of curves produced by cutting through a cone, or the study of these curves.

conjecture An unproven theorem.

cosine The ratio of the side adjacent to an angle to the hypotenuse in a right-angled triangle.

differential calculus (differentiation) Method for calculating the slope of a curve at a particular point.

Diophantine equation An equation in which all the numbers involved are whole numbers.

fractal A curve or other figure that repeats its overall pattern or shape in portions of constantly reducing size, so that a portion of the figure when magnified looks the same as the whole figure.

function A mathematical expression with one or more variables.

geometry The branch of mathematics concerned with the properties of points, lines, and shapes that exist in one, two, three, or more dimensions.

hyperbola A curve produced by slicing through a cone with a plane with a smaller angle at its axis than the side of the cone.

imaginary number A number that involves the square root of -1.

infinitesimal Very small quantity, tending toward zero.

integral The product of integration.

integral calculus (**integration**) Method of calculating the area under a curve by approximating the sum of a large number of infinitely thin slices of the area.

limit The lowest or highest value to which a function will be calculated.

logarithm The power to which a base figure (usually 10 or e) must be raised to give a specified number.

optics The study of lenses, vision, and light.

parabola Curve produced by slicing through a cone with a plane parallel to the side of the cone.

perpendicular At right angles to.

polynomial equation An equation that involves non-zero powers of a variable (e.g. $x^2 + 4x + 1 = 0$).

quadratic equation An equation of the form $ax^2 + bx + c = 0$.

rational number A number that can be expressed as a ratio of two whole numbers.

real number Any positive or negative number that does not involve the square root of -1.

set Related group of entities.

sexagesimal Base 60.

sine The ratio of the side opposite an angle to the hypotenuse in a right-angled triangle.

tangent The ratio of the side opposite an angle to the side adjacent to the angle in a right-angled triangle.

theorem Statement of a rule that is not self-evident but which can be proven by logical steps.

topology The study of geometric properties that are not affected by changes of shape or size.

torus A surface formed by revolving a circle in three-dimensional space around a point that does not intersect it. The shape of a torus is similar to a ring shaped doughnut.

transfinite numbers Numbers that relate to infinities of different magnitudes; so the infinite number of whole numbers is smaller than the infinite number of real numbers.

trigonometry The mathematical study of the angles and sides of triangles and their relationships.

For Further Reading

Crilly, Tony. *50 Mathematical Ideas You Really Need to Know.* New York, NY: Quercus, 2008.

Dyson, George. *Turing's Cathedral: The Origins of the Digital Universe.* New York, NY: Pantheon, 2012.

Pickover, Clifford A. *The Math Book: From Pythagoras to the 57th Dimension, 250 Milestones in the History of Mathematics.* New York, NY: Sterling Publishing, 2012.

Stewart, Ian. *In Pursuit of the Unknown: 17 Equations That Changed the World.* New York, NY: Basic Books, 2012.

Web Sites

Due to the changing nature of Internet links, Rosen Publishing has developed an online list of Web sites related to the subject of this book. This site is updated regularly. Please use this link to access the list:

http://www.rosenlinks.com/gph/mathe

Index

Acknowledgments

Picture Credits
Key: b. = bottom, t. = top, l. = left, r. = right, c. = center

Art Archive (Picture Desk): 7
Bridgeman Art Library: 18, 41 (b.l.), 77
Clipart: 21, 22, 27 (t.r.)
Corbis: 15, 26, 27 (t.l.), 38, 58 (b.l.), 60, 65 (t.l.), 66, 73, 91, 93 (t.l.), 98, 106, 108 (t.l.), 114, 115, 121, 123
Dr James R Warren: 40
Getty: 64 (b.l.), 70, 83
Picture Desk/The Art Archive: 56
RIA Novosti: 30
Science Photo Library: 35, 46 (b.l.), 51, 52 (b.l.), 104, 112, 118
Shutterstock: 23, 81
Topfoto: 29 (b.c.), 88 (b.l. & r.), 116
Wikimedia: Wolfgang Beyer: 119

Diagrams: David Woodroffe

We have endeavored to contact the copyright-holders of all images used in this book. Any oversights in this regard will be rectified in future editions.